THOUGHTLANDS

THOUGHTLANDS

WALKING IN WRITERS' SUFFOLK

Jacky Colliss Harvey

First published by Armchair Traveller in 2026
An imprint of Haus Publishing Ltd.
4 Cinnamon Row, London SW11 3TW

www.hauspublishing.com

A CIP catalogue for this book is available from the British Library

ISBN 978-1-914982-18-7
eISBN 978-1-914982-19-4

Typeset in Garamond by MacGuru Ltd
Printed in Suffolk, UK by Clays Ltd (Elcograf S.p.A.)

Map on pages vi and vii designed by Rhys Davies
Route maps and sketches by Jacky Colliss Harvey
With thanks to Faber & Faber Ltd for permission to use the excerpt on page 130

The authorised representative in the EEA is:
Haus Publishing, Casella Postale 32
50037 San Piero a Sieve (Fi), Italy
gpsr@hauspublishing.com

MIX
Paper | Supporting responsible forestry
FSC® C018072
FSC
www.fsc.org

This one is for my dad.

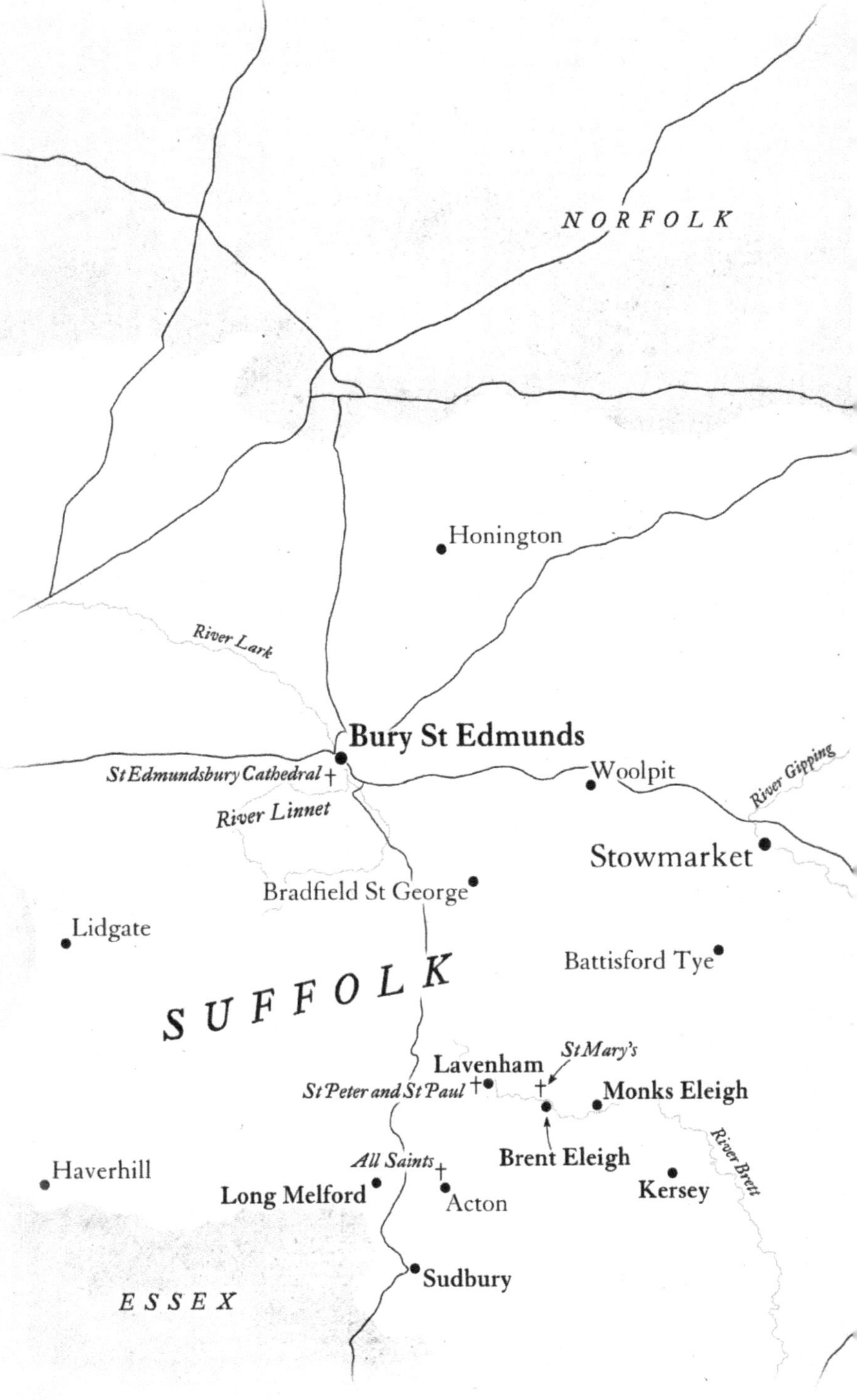
NORFOLK
Honington
River Lark
Bury St Edmunds
St Edmundsbury Cathedral
Woolpit
River Gipping
River Linnet
Stowmarket
Bradfield St George
Lidgate
Battisford Tye
SUFFOLK
St Mary's
Lavenham
St Peter and St Paul
Monks Eleigh
River Brett
Brent Eleigh
All Saints
Haverhill
Long Melford
Acton
Kersey
Sudbury
ESSEX

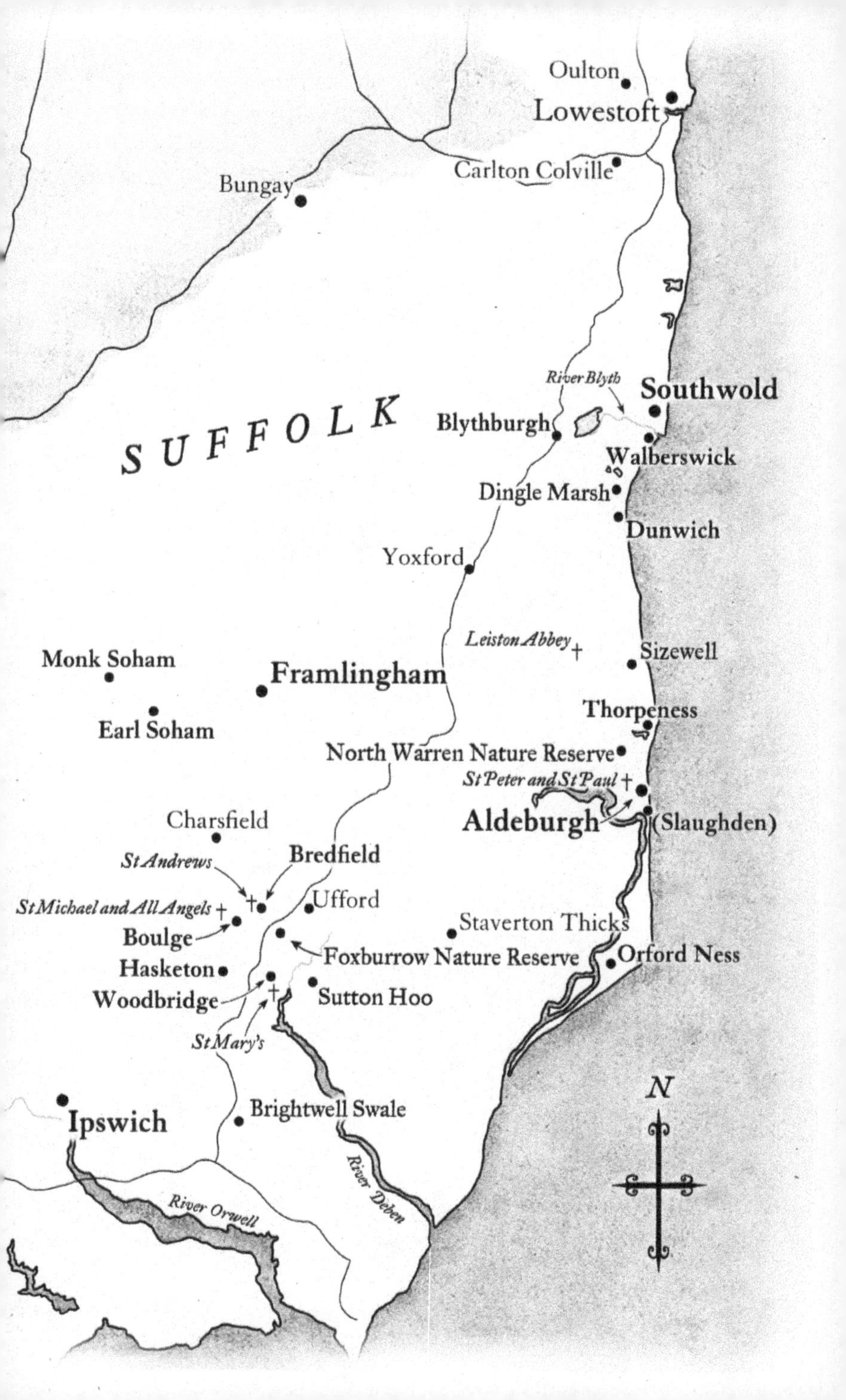
Oulton
Lowestoft
Carlton Colville
Bungay
SUFFOLK
River Blyth
Southwold
Blythburgh
Walberswick
Dingle Marsh
Dunwich
Yoxford
Leiston Abbey
Sizewell
Monk Soham
Framlingham
Earl Soham
Thorpeness
North Warren Nature Reserve
St Peter and St Paul
Aldeburgh
(Slaughden)
Charsfield
St Andrews
Bredfield
St Michael and All Angels
Ufford
Boulge
Staverton Thicks
Foxburrow Nature Reserve
Orford Ness
Hasketon
Woodbridge
Sutton Hoo
St Mary's
N
Brightwell Swale
Ipswich
River Deben
River Orwell

Contents

Introduction

> 'A man must have thought much over scenery before he begins fully to enjoy it.'
>
> Robert Louis Stevenson

SUFFOLK. The abode of the 'South folk', just as Norfolk was that of the 'North folk'. You have to love the economy of effort of those first Anglo-Saxon namers of names. 'Angle' is there in the root of the word 'England', too; and is the crux of the story of a papal pun ascribed to Gregory I, bishop of Rome from 590 to 604. Spying a huddle of child-slaves for sale in a market in Rome, he is supposed to have asked about their blond hair, and been told they were *Anglii*. 'Yes,' Gregory is meant to have replied, 'they look like angels, too.'

I too am a Suffolk child, a 'tractor girl', so-called, a phrase I trace back to 1978, when Ipswich Town played Arsenal in the final of the FA Cup. Ipswich were very much the underdogs, and a cartoon appeared in *The Telegraph* that morning. It showed Wembley Stadium in the background, and in the foreground two signs, one pointing left and one right: 'Car Park' and the other 'Tractor Park'. (*Miraculo Dei*, Ipswich won.) I have always felt more Suffolk than English, or any other designation. Place me anywhere with a low horizon and huge skies – Venice, for example, or the Isle of Dogs, where I live now – and I am immediately at home. James Rebanks, in *The Shepherd's Life*, talks of sheep being 'hefted', of having a sense of where their place is, of coming back to that particular place on the fell as part of their comprehension of themselves. My parents came from the West Country, but I am hefted to Suffolk. My personal altimeter was calibrated to that landscape flat as a biscuit, that cathedral vault of a sky, while I was still in my cot; it is not going to change now.

Suffolk. Which is an obstacle course of furrows of ploughed earth high enough to have to be lifted over, when you are a tot; which is verges a-flop with nettles and cow-parsley and hedges spiked with hawthorn; which is unreliable buses rattling down country lanes and black-top roads that meander through the green, green, green – every shade of green, an explosion of viridescence, as if the trees were burning with leaf. Which is history that jumps out of nowhere and grabs you like a mugger. Which is fields like nuclear wastelands and shingle underfoot, aching calves and Adnams beer; friendly rivers, hungry sea; stands of anorexic pines on pre-Roman tumuli, dripping in the rain; and the glorious fractal universe of some shaggy Tudor oak, standing sentinel at the place where four fields meet. Hideously ugly town centres and churches lovely enough to have even the most uncompromising unbeliever wonder if there isn't something to it, something there. Old Suffolk: home to Sutton Hoo, and long before that, the Neolithic fisher-folk who sat in what became the field beside my parents' house and shucked oysters from the River Deben, throwing the shells behind them into a chalky pile and ringing their fire with stones that reddened and blackened in the heat, and then reappeared in streaks of stuttering light and dark in the chop-through of the earth, of history itself, that was the side of the irrigation ditch our local farmer dug across that same field during the drought of 1976. History is always there. It sits beneath you, waiting.

Then there is the visitor's Suffolk, the 'newcomes' Suffolk, of half-timbering and plaster-pargeting, colour-washed with Suffolk pink – lime-wash and ox-blood and take your pick: powdered brick, or maybe the juice of sloe and elderberries, or onion skins, or who knows what, that begins as a colour so vivid it shouts at the eyeballs, and weathers down to the tubercular tint of a wilting rose. Spoken Suffolk, an accent now so rare that when I hear it, it turns me around in the street; an accent like cobnuts being rolled down a tray; a shove-ha'penny accent that shrugs off anything it doesn't need – assorted consonants, the i-n-g of a gerund (in Suffolk, 'ing' is invariably 'un'); creating an end result in which perhaps you still hear the Jutland peninsula, the original *Anglii*, even today. With Proust, it was crumbs in a spoon, with me, it is three words: 'Yeorrrroightbor?' (There truly are three words in there, however it might appear.) 'Non-rhotic' is the phonetic term for the Suffolk accent, and you hear it in eastern *New* England, too. The first syllable of this compound Suffolk watchword is typically pronounced very slowly, like an engine firing up, and that habitual slow firing-up has had its effect on the Suffolk sense of humour, too, which is slyly self-aware and ironical, and has a profound appreciation of punchlines. As a little girl I remember watching the village window-cleaner going about his task of transforming our windows from dusty, rain-spotted glass to magical invisibility. As I watched, my beloved ginger tomcat, Freddy (a cat of Buddha-like good humour, and Persian amounts of fur, though his origin was no grander than a barn up the road), wandered into view, then dropped to the ground, in apparent exhaustion. The window-cleaner paused, and gave Freddy a long, considered look. 'Thass worroi mean,' he said, stooping to wring out his cloth. ''E do rush abeowt so.' 'Yod-dropping', which sounds like pub game in itself, is another characteristic of the Suffolk accent, and is the reason why a friend's nephew spoke of working in an IT lesson at school on his 'pooter'. We give our words due attention, we South Folk. As described in *Akenfield*, Ronald Blythe's chronicle of Suffolk life, we are a serious people who laugh a lot.

And then there is written Suffolk. Robert Louis Stevenson, he of *Treasure Island*, was here in July 1873, writing to his mother: 'Yesterday we were away to Melford and Lavenham, both exceptionally placid, beautiful old English towns. Melford scattered all round a big green, with an Elizabethan Hall and Park, great screens of trees that seem twice as high as trees should seem ...' Stevenson was doing finger-exercises, if you like, for his essay 'Roads', in which he speaks of a road that 'rolls upon the easy slopes of the country, like a long ship in the hollows of the sea.' Sutton Hoo and its great ship-burial, last resting place (perhaps) of Rædwald, one of the first kings of the East Angles, was uncovered only in 1938, so Stevenson was not thinking of that, but when he wrote 'Roads', he had Suffolk in mind, without a doubt. The connection between the Angles and those long ships has been a part of history since at least the seventh-century chronicler we know as the Venerable Bede: 'the nation of the Angles, or Saxons ... arrived in Britain with three ships of war and had a place in which to settle assigned to them ... in the eastern part of the island.'

Sheep have their sheep tracks, we have our roads, on which we walked, and walk, from where we are to where we want to be. We walked out of Africa, when the biggest of us would not have been much taller than a seven-year-old child, with our heads raised, scanning our new grassland surroundings for all those creatures so much larger and stronger than us, and for which we would be no more than lunch. We walked on our new, longer, straighter big toes, the fulcrum on which our feet lift at the ankle and go forward, heel down, into the next step. We walked with our front legs, now our arms, dangling in front of us, ready to discover the skills of foraging and gathering, of farming and hunting, of holding and nursing, of making and transforming, and ultimately, of writing too. We walked with our pelvises at a different tilt and with our upright, S-shaped spines protecting more of our bodies from the heat of the sun and supporting our ridiculously oversized heads that were such a damn problem to squeeze out through those pelvises in the first place, whilst we scanned and hunted and held and made, and at some point maybe 300,000 years into our onward walk, all that scanning and hunting and holding and making began to give us the brains we have today, with their tyrannical demands for energy and care and cosmos-sized capacities to plan, to invent, to imagine; to do what I am doing in writing this and you are doing in reading it. The point is, we were built to do this. Walking is a driver, maybe *the* driver in our evolution; that great walk is still continuing, still there in all our walks, and the electrical circuit between walking and thinking and writing is one that has been with us for a very long time indeed.

Suffolk is good walking country. Robert Reyce, in his *Breviary of Suffolk* of 1618, described it as 'delighting in a continual evenness and plainness ... void of any great hills, high mountains, or steep rocks.' In other words, you may walk it without needing to give all your attention to the walking. Edward Moor, another Suffolk native, who published *Suffolk Words and Phrases* in 1823, lists 'a-walking' as being a specific vernacular form of the verb, denoting a continuance of action. As you a-walk, you fall into what Rebecca Solnit, the uber-walker of our time, has described as 'an observer's state, cool, withdrawn, with senses sharpened, a good state for anybody who needs to reflect or create.' The one-two rhythm of easeful walking becomes the beat of the walker's heart – and (or so it has always seemed to me) that of iambic pentameter, too. Like an infant in a sling, the monkey-brain puts its thumb in its mouth and is soothed and quietened. Or as Stevenson puts it, 'once you have fallen into an equable stride, it requires no conscious thought from you to keep it up, and yet it prevents you from thinking earnestly of anything else. Like knitting ... it gradually neutralises and sets to sleep the serious activity of the mind.' The mind, lulled, gives us mindfulness. When you walk, you are in a constant present, moving within a continual here and now – the past is invisible behind you, the future, literally ahead. Walking, we fill the moment. We know exactly where we are, and even though we are in continual motion, in each moment, we are still. Walking in country as flat as Suffolk there are times when it can seem as if you are the spindle on an old-fashioned record-player and the landscape is in motion around you, not you within it at all: distant roofs, stands of trees, church spires, slide toward you like scenery being pushed about in a toy theatre, move away, then re-appear, and rarely where expected. In *The Rings of Saturn*, his extraordinary account of East Anglian walking, W. G. Sebald speaks of how, travelling inland from Dunwich (where we will also tread), he felt as if he was being followed by 'a most peculiar villa, with a glass-domed observation tower' which appeared 'time and again ... now close to, now further off, now to my left and now to my right,' and how

> ... indeed at one point the look-out tower, in a sort of castling move, had got itself, in no time at all from one side of the building to the other, so that it seemed that instead of seeing the actual villa I was seeing its mirror image.

That is what this landscape, these flats of Suffolk do: they play chess with you, and you cannot talk about walking in and writing about and thinking of Suffolk at all without feeling Sebald's gentle ghost standing quietly there behind you. When he began (and begins) his book, in August 1992, he had set off 'to walk the county of Suffolk, in the hope of dispelling the emptiness that takes hold of me whenever I have completed a long stint of work.' A mere 7,000 steps a day (which, come on, is no more than the running of an errand) is, according to the *New Scientist*, enough to lower your risk of developing heart disease, depression, and dementia, indeed of dying from any cause whatsoever. The hippocampus – that little sea-horse-shaped structure in the centre of the brain, and at the centre of everything the brain has to do (forming thoughts, forming memories, forming writing, and so on), which shrivels like a walnut in its shell at the onset of such disorders as Alzheimer's – thrives on walking: the new sights being processed, the new experiences, the oxygen in deeper breaths. Its volume increases. It is hydrated with BDNF, or 'brain-derived neurotrophic factor', crucial for neuroplasticity, which is the brain's ability to rewire itself, to adapt, to keep going as it should. In every way it can, walking recharges you, like running the engine to charge the battery in a car. Or as Solnit puts it:

> The rhythm of walking generates a kind of rhythm of thinking, and the passage through a landscape ... stimulates the passage through a series of thoughts. This creates an odd consonance between internal and external passage, one that suggests that the mind is also a landscape of sorts and that walking is one way to traverse it.

I do wish Solnit weren't so good at this sort of thing; she makes it almost pointless for any other writer to attempt to describe what goes on up there within the easeful rhythm of a walk. But still, we try. In *Flâneuse: Women Walk the City*, Lauren Elkin talks of 'the utter total freedom unleashed from the act of putting one foot in front of the other,' and the 'liberating possibilities of a good walk.' Exactly. There is absolute autonomy in walking. Leave the unmade bed, the unstacked dishwasher, the imperious demands of the inbox, all that; pull on a pair of friendly shoes, get out that door and walk. When I found myself living on my own for the first time since university, it was in Pimlico, and despite the cack-handedness of the post-war conversion of my rented flat, which resulted in rooms higher than they were wide, and the fact that the time I spent within them was made ridiculous by illness, I loved living there. It was the first place the Yankee came to stay with me, to begin with (you will hear more of him), but the other reason I so relished my time there is that after years of living ever further and further away from the centre of London, and needing to catch a train to go and do *anything*, in Pimlico, if I wanted to be anywhere, all I had to do was walk out the door and I was on my way. Walking is one of those things you do by doing it. Like writing, in fact.

Years ago, I heard what I remembered as a clip from a French radio interview with A. S. Byatt, where she spoke about the process of writing *The Whistling Woman*. At least, I thought I remembered having heard it, as for months I was wholly unable to find any such interview, despite all my dragnetting for it online. This was deeply annoying, as the memory of it was one of the starting points for my thinking about this book, since it included so perfect an example of the connection there is between thinking and walking and writing. Finally, I decided that I would reconstruct the interview, as far as I could, from memory, and include it in this book in the hopes that someone reading its description would direct me toward the real thing – if it existed at all. Then up it popped – the A. S. Byatt episode of the series *Scribbling*: not a radio interview at all, but a TV programme broadcast in 2002 on BBC2. Fifteen minutes in, Byatt leaves her house in France and goes for a walk. 'Up to about here,' she says, indicating the approaching house, 'all I do is stop all the things I'm worried about ... By this corner, an image of some bit of the novel will come into my head. By the next corner, I will usually have had an idea.' The camera retreats. On she goes, walking steadily past us, along a path through trees. Her voice remains: 'The thinking gets better the more I get this very steady rhythm.' Solnit would agree: 'My circuit was almost finished,' she writes of one of her regular routes, 'and at the end of it I knew what my subject was and how to address it in a way I had not six miles before.' That horror, writer's block, is not a block at all, or at least has never felt so to me: it is not one thing obstructing a writer's creativity or imagination, it is too many, a logjam of words and ideas all fighting against and blocking each other. Go for a walk. The logjam will unjam itself; the ideas get into an orderly queue. You cannot be blocked when you are in motion. Aristotle and his students walked up and down and thought and talked in the Lyceum in Athens, and no doubt the trick was discovered long before them. Keep walking, for you will inevitably arrive. The philosopher Frédéric Gros speaks of thoughts born in walking as thoughts 'born of movement,' in which you can feel rhythm, lightness, freedom. 'During that continuous but automatic effort of the body,' he tells us, 'the mind is placed at one's disposal.' Friedrich Nietzsche, an obsessive walker and one of the first and loudest voices in Gros's *A Philosophy of Walking*, held that the only good writing was that done with the feet. Walking is good writing country, in other words. By contrast the landscape of memory, remaking itself over and over again, is like the countryside in *Alice Through the Looking-Glass*, where gardens transform into wildernesses, hills might be valleys, bees become elephants, and all of it is a giant chessboard governed by rules that rewrite themselves continuously.

This is another thing our cosmos-sized minds enable us to do: to think of one thing in terms of another. Thus, a journey – any journey, an undertaking with a beginning and an end – becomes a metaphor for an individual life, or in the case of John Bunyan's great allegory *The Pilgrim's Progress*, the progress of a soul. But it only works one way. You will not be the same person on any journey back as you were on the journey going forth. Vachel Lindsay, who declaimed his poetry from the stage, striding back and forth like a carnival barker, wrote in his 'Singing Poetry' of 1929:

> We met ourselves as we came back,
> And were happy in mist and rain.
> Our old souls and our new souls
> Met to salute and explain—

In the movie of Ronald Blythe's *Akenfield: Portrait of an English Village*, the character of Old Tom is still pondering in voiceover – perhaps from beyond the grave – what he could have been 'if I hadn't a-walked the forty mile back from Newmarket,' where he went as a young man in search of a better job, a better life, a better, bigger, anything. Everyone I knew went to watch Peter Hall's movie of *Akenfield* when it came out in 1974. I still remember my astonishment at seeing Suffolk, my place, *home*, up there on the big screen, for everyone in the whole world to have a look at, but I remember also the tears of recognition in my mother's eyes at Old Tom's words, the powerful, painful way they clearly spoke to her. As a child it never occurs to you that mothers might regret their choices, but they do; like all of us, of course they do, and like all of us have to make peace with the fact that we are not designed to go backwards. No-one can ever truly retrace their steps, the same steps they took before; any more than as the proverb puts it, you can step twice in the same river, or than two people will read the same book and take away the same sense of it. All travel cannot but be travel forward, and travel forward is mortality. A treasured mentor died as I was working on this book; the first from my generation in my circle of friends died too, arriving at the end of his thread with no warning and far too soon; and one icy January night I took a tumble down a set of dockyard steps, heard the crunch as I landed (and hearing that inner crunch is never good), and just before the pain of it roared up my leg, thought 'I've bust my ankle,' and so I had. I was no longer spry enough to bounce. There are now exercises that must be done every morning; there are parts of my body that were once obediently silent, which now give voice to surly complaint if I neglect them. My tree has rings, and I too have regrets.

*

This is a book is about walking and writing: about walkers who wrote, and writers who walk. And because it is a book about walking and writing it is also a book about thinking, that circuit between mind and feet, and about moving through a landscape that can be both physically in front of you, and exist in a line of words or the flight of a line of thought. It is also a book about Suffolk, where I come from as a writer. It has something in it of the journal and the writer's notebook; a little of the memoir and of the love-letter, too. It is a literary biography of a landscape, and although I hope it speaks out wider than my own experience, it is inevitably curated. This is a word so overused these days that you feel you almost have to put it in quote marks to protect it, but despite the gravity with which it is so often pronounced and the number of poor choices it so often hides, all it really means is this is who and what interests me and why, and I offer it up with the humble wish it may divert and interest you, too, that we may share. It has, therefore a cast: characters both major and minor, among them Ronald Blythe, George Ewart Evans, W. G. Sebald, M. R. James, and Hammond Innes; George Crabbe, Daniel Defoe, Robert Bloomfield and Edward FitzGerald; Maggie Hemingway, P. D. James,

Penelope Fitzgerald, Norah Lofts, and 'Ouida'. It also features William Alfred Dutt (1870–1939), who curated his own *Literary Associations of East Anglia*, and of it, wrote:

> All I can claim to have done is to have gathered together a number of facts, anecdotes, and incidents, together with certain opinions and impressions of East Anglia; to have connected them as nearly as possible with the places they in a greater or lesser degree belong to; and to have tried to give some sort of form to a rather rambling subject ...

In her study of women walking, Lauren Elkin created the persona of the *flâneuse*, the female stroller, the woman who walks the city. I am laying claim here to the *rambleuse*, the woman who walks the countryside, alert for incidents and impressions and those flighting lines of thought that come from walking, but especially from walking where other writers have walked before; the network of associations thrown over a landscape that you feel stretching above your head like lines of music, or like the vines and tendrils of an arbour; a metaphysical mathematics that can bring one and one together and make of them three. 'I have traced a path which I will follow,' said Immanuel Kant, another daily walker, in eighteenth-century Konigsberg, and I will endeavour to do the same – from west to east, from cathedral city to open fields, from velvety farmlands muffled by leaves to deafening shingle and darkening sea. Because if, as the artist Paul Klee said, drawing is taking a line for a walk, then writing is doing the same with a thought. And as Florence Green asks herself, out in the Suffolk fields in Penelope Fitzgerald's *The Bookshop*, what else can be done with flatlands but to cross them?

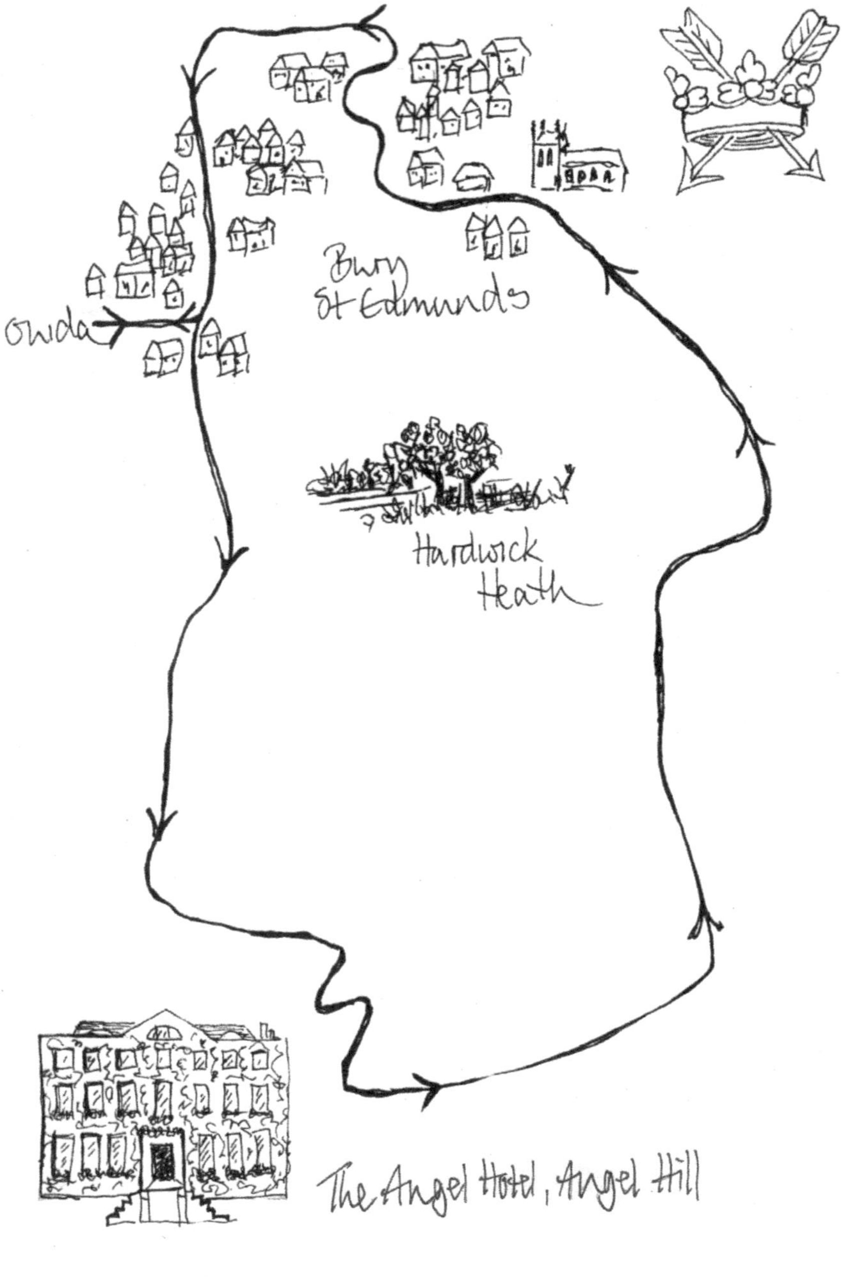
Bury
St Edmunds
Ouida
Hardwick
Heath
The Angel Hotel, Angel Hill

1

Patron Saints

Bury St Edmunds

THE PATRON SAINT of the humble foot and ankle is St Servatius, who is meant to have died of a leg wound. He is also one of the 'Ice Saints', in that his feast day, 13 May, sometimes coincides with the last frosts of the year. It is probably only me who puts the idea of an Ice Saint and an injured limb together. The patron saint of broken bones is the sixteenth-century St Stanislaus Kostka, possibly because he suffered more than a few of them at the hands of his brother Paul. Of walkers, it is St James the Great, of the great Camino de Santiago pilgrimage trail. Writers have a choice of four: Filippo Neri, Francis de Sales, Teresa d'Ávila (from whose remains the attentions of the faithful have, since her death in 1582, removed both hands, one arm, her upper jaw, her right foot, her left eye and her heart – a metaphor for how one puts oneself into one's writing, perhaps), and the twelfth-century abbess Hildegard of Bingen. The latter had visions, and described herself as not hearing them 'with my outward ears, nor do I perceive them by the thoughts of my own heart or by any combination of my five senses, but in my soul alone, while my outward eyes are open'. This is very striking. Writing requires a lot of co-ordinated activity in several parts of the brain, one of which inevitably is the hippocampus, which both stores and retrieves memories, but another is the area of the visual cortex, suggesting that when you write, you are describing something that you inwardly 'see'. A third part of the brain that seems to be involved is 'Broca's area' in the left frontal lobe; this part of the brain is important not for vision, but for speech. Sometimes when you write you see the story, like a movie. Sometimes you hear it, as if it were being narrated to you. In my experience, the two feel completely different. It's worth noting that there is more activity in the speech-centred part of the writing brain in those who write daily, like me, than there is in those who are just starting out. The same is true for the 'caudate nucleus', which sits hunkered down on top of the hippocampus like a biker over his Kawasaki, and fires up when you perform an action you have done many times before. In other words, Hildegarde's account of her visions could be taken as the experience of watching your brain at work as you write, and is probably as good a description of that inward process as one could hope for. It moves forward, it takes a path, one scene, or one word, after another.

There is sadly no patron saint for those such as me, born

with almost no sense of direction whatsoever (you have been warned), but perhaps that is how it should be. No, for us, these days, there is GPS and the mobile phone. You are, however, more than a blue dot on a map. I have never been able to understand those who walk without lifting their heads from their phones and looking about them – what is the point of walking, if you don't do that?

The patron saint of Suffolk is of course St Edmund the Martyr. Before he was a saint, Edmund was a king of the Angles, who had by now forgotten all about their time in those three ships of war and been settled in their eastern kingdom for generations. But where one ship finds its way, others will as well, and the 'Great Heathen Army' arrived from Scandinavia in 865. Legend has it that Edmund died at their hands in 869, a type of Suffolk St Sebastian, tied to a tree and pierced with arrows as numerous as the bristles on a hedgehog – or so the monk Ælfric of Eynsham described it the following century. Edmund was then beheaded. His attackers left his body where it fell, but threw the head into a ditch, where it was guarded by a wolf – a wolf grown tame, because in John Lydgate's later telling of the legend, nothing is impossible with God. Lydgate (*c.*1370–*c.*1451) was a local boy, from the village of Lidgate 10 miles (16 kilometres) away, so obviously his account can be trusted implicitly. Robert Reyce in his *Breviary* describes him as 'a monke in the abbey of Bury, an excellent poet, yea the chiefe as was supposed in this science for that age.' Lydgate neglects to mention where

St Edmund's martyrdom took place, but folk belief (and Ronald Blythe) opts for the woods at 'Staverton Thicks', almost 40 miles (65 kilometres) away toward the coast. If a wolf crept out from between the great dropsical trunks of the ancient, pollarded oaks of Staverton Thicks I would not be surprised even today. Just as now, once it was safe to do so, people went out to retrieve the bodies of the fallen, but they could not find King Edmund's head until it called out to them 'I am here, I am here!' A saint, in that case, from the word go, and it would seem he was already being venerated as such within a couple of decades of his death. The abbey that ultimately housed his shrine, in the town that came to be known as Bury St Edmunds in his honour, grew into one of the wealthiest pilgrimage sites in all England.

Bury St Edmunds is posh. It is most definitely upper-middle: lots of ABC1s. It was posh in 1724, when Daniel Defoe walked or more likely rode through it, wearing his reportage hat (as opposed to that in which he gave us *Robinson Crusoe* and *Moll Flanders)*. In his *Tour Thro' the Whole Island of Great Britain* he called it 'the Montpellier of Suffolk', for its 'pleasant situation and wholesome air.' Bury was where my school, in Ipswich, came for day trips, introducing us schoolgirls to monks and medieval history and the gigantic abbey ruins, because we had nothing like that at home, where the old centre of the town had been knocked flat and buried under concrete. 'Of Ipswich,' says M. R. James in his 1930 *Suffolk and Norfolk*, 'it is not my intention to say much.' Certainly we had no great saintly shrine, so large and strongly built that even Henry VIII's commissioners found it 'very cumbrous' to throw down. Indeed, the two towns seem always to have always understood which was blue collar and which was white. The journalist William Cobbett, in his *Rural Rides* of 1822–6, records in amazement how

> ... even at Ipswich, when I was praising *that place*, the very people of that town asked me if I did not think Bury St. Edmund's the nicest town in the world. Meet them wherever you will, they have all the same boast; and indeed, as a town *in itself*, it is the neatest place that ever was seen. It is airy, it has several fine open places in it, and it has the remains of the famous abbey walls and the abbey gate entire; and it is so clean and so neat that nothing can equal it in that respect.

Others have been more circumspect. It was, said William Dutt,

> ... a self-centred, self-reliant town. Contentedly, it devotes itself to its own interests, but lags in the wake of progress. The chief town of West Suffolk, it has no ambition to wider distinction than its past has given it and its present maintains; consequently, we find it more concerned about the precise location of an abbot's tomb than in schemes of modern improvement.

Those of us who knew Ipswich at its worst may well think Bury was the one with its priorities right.

Such a mindset does not suit all. The novelist Ouida (Maria Louise Ramé), who was born in Bury in 1839 and fled it as soon as she could, infamously said of her birthplace that it 'always puts me in the mind of an old maid dressed for a party ... Why, the inhabitants are driven to ringing their own door-bells lest they rust from lack of use.' She called it a 'little owl of a town,' although it seems to have been lucky for woman writers. Before Ouida there was Elizabeth Inchbald (1753–1821), so stagestruck that despite a stammer she determined upon a career in the theatre, first as an actress and later as a playwright, and later still, as a novelist, although just like their creator, her heroes, brothers William and Henry, have to walk away from home (which must also sometimes be done) before their story can begin.

> As they walked out of their native town, each with a small bundle at his back, each observed the other drop several tears: but, upon the sudden meeting of their eyes, they both smiled with a degree of disdain at the weakness in which they had been caught.
>
> 'I am sure,' said William (the elder), 'I don't know what makes me cry.'
>
> 'Nor I neither,' said Henry; 'for though we may never see this town again, yet we leave nothing behind us to give us reason to lament.'

'No,' replied William, 'nor anybody who cares what becomes of us.'

The novelist Norah Lofts (the antidote, if you like, to Inchbald and Ouida), spent her whole life in Bury St Edmunds, and all the inspiration for her many books came from its streets and its history. Dickens was here too, of course, first as journalist in 1835 and then as the most famous writer in England in 1859 and 1861. He stayed at the Angel Inn, now the Angel Hotel, and brought Mr Pickwick with him. 'A handsome little town,' Dickens called it, 'of thriving and cleanly appearance,' with 'a large inn situated in a wide open street, nearly facing the old abbey.' (He was very specific about Bury, whereas he hid nearby Sudbury's identity as 'Eatanswill'.) Edward FitzGerald, the translator of the Victorian literary sensation *The Rubaiyat of Omar Khayyam* went to school here, when the King Edward VI School was in Northgate Street; 'now used as a girl's school,' says William Dutt, dismissively, although not the same as that where Mr Pickwick had his midnight misadventures, attempting to thwart a non-existent elopement. Lucy Barton (also not that one), briefly FitzGerald's wife, was to comment of her husband's school days that 'if among his school-fellows flourished any embryo Apollo he would have temporarily constituted the youth his heart's idol,' thus laying out perfectly clearly – but with lady-like restraint – why their marriage was such a disaster, and tying up in one sentence what FitzGerald's contemporary male biographers, Dutt included, would tie themselves in knots to obfuscate and hide.

Ruth Rendell, in her darker persona as Barbara Vine, used Bury in *The Brimstone Wedding*, contrasting its well-to-do gentrified air with the desperation of the lives lived behind its handsome Georgian facades, and the size of the town itself with the smallness and isolation of the villages around it. Genevieve, or Jenny, the heroine of *The Brimstone Wedding*, lives a life she wants to leave in a house for which she feels nothing: 'just a house Mike and I had bought on a mortgage, not because we liked it but because it was all we could afford, not in a place we chose but the only place we knew. Most of the people I know lived like that'. Stella, her elderly counterpart within the plot, had lived with her solicitor husband in a house that epitomised his professional success, but which was just as wretchedly miserable. You can go along almost any street in the centre of Bury and see the kind of house I mean – flat fronted, sash windowed, pediment impressively high, and these days, more often than not, a solicitor's office – but don't be fooled. There is a deal more to Bury than might at first meet the eye.

*

There are differing schools of thought where walking in company is concerned. The walker in pursuit of the epic demands that walks should be taken – undertaken – on one's own. Company would be cheating; to be solitary, alone with your own thinking for as long as possible, is the whole point. For Cheryl Strayed, in *Wild*, walking the Pacific Crest Trail on her own was a means of making manifest the loneliness and emptiness she sensed within her life, of luring the dragon out in order to slay it. Two hundred years before Cheryl Strayed set out, William Hazlitt was making a similar case in his essay 'On Going a Journey': 'The soul of a journey is liberty, perfect liberty, to think, feel, do just as one pleases'. The presence of company changes this: 'In setting out on a party of pleasure, the first consideration always is where we shall go to: in taking a solitary ramble, the question is what we shall meet with by the way'. He allowed that a companion could be a pleasant thing to have only when a walk was coming to its end, and you wanted to discuss what you might have for dinner. The *rambleuse*, however, does not care to be solitary. I like a companion when I walk, so long as it is one who moves at the same pace as me, whose conversation sparks into life at the same time as mine does, who falls silent at the same time, too. It is an excellent test of a friendship: is this someone you could pull a sled with, if you had to? Twin and I were finishing each other's sentences within five minutes of our first meeting, twenty years ago; we have been friends ever since, and if, while walking, we were to find ourselves pulling away from each other (her stride is even longer than mine), we had Hans to bustle along between us and link us together again. I should describe Hans. Hans is what an AI would come up with if instructed to create a dog that reminds everyone who sees him of their beloved first teddy bear. If all else failed, we also had Merlin, the Cornell University bird-identification app, to which Twin and I are equally addicted.

Of this walk, however, what I was looking for was contrast: two of the landscapes that typify Suffolk – the market town and the meadows and fields around it – then a curl back into Bury and a mooch around the abbey ruins and the graveyard. Writers love graveyards. They are such wonderful places to go hunting for names, to begin with, for names and for stories. Gravestones are like writing exercises. One reads the bare facts of born, of died, of loss and the command comes as from some unseen tutor: *make a story out of this*. I know this is ghoulish, but so are we. I wanted to see where Norah Lofts lived (this, for a writer, is what touching the relics of a saint must be for those of faith), and where Ouida was born, to relive those trips here with my school, and to see if the buildings of Bury still had that particular way of sitting under its trees and if its ivy-covered flint walls still reminded me as immediately of seaweedy mussel beds. I wanted an easy way into this book that would brush lightly against its themes and preoccupations without setting them ringing like tubular bells, and which might serve as a warning to any reader who found themselves on what felt like the wrong path that they could turn around now. I wanted something long but not too long – 5 or 6 miles or so – especially since we were walking at the time of year when summer, having faded in its own bright light, peels off to reveal autumn. I wanted to get down to the River Linnet and the River Lark, as who can know a River Linnet and a River Lark exist and not want to walk beside them, but it seemed wise not to trust the elements too far. Especially when that paler sky above us was skeiny with cloud, of the sort that suggests very soon the big Suffolk sky, with all the space it leaves above your head for thought and dreaming and imagining, would shortly descend thousands of metres and sit above us solid as kapok and as heavy as a migraine, 'a huge lid', as *The Brimstone Wedding* has it, and as Baudelaire described the pressure of such a sky in Paris, too, in his poem 'Spleen' from *Les Fleurs du Mal* of 1857, creating 'a daylight dingier than dark'. Such is the yin to the yang of the Suffolk cloud-base: the meteorological price we pay. The day was moving on. It was time for us to do so too. Let us walk.

*

We began at the Angel, turned our back on the Abbey, and headed for Northgate Street, and found Norah Lofts's house immediately, all four mighty brick bays of it. It alarmed me that it looked as if so large a house had now been chopped up into council offices, but *Country Life* assures me it is still a home, albeit one with its lovely Georgian plasterwork and corniced doorways painted in the archetypal palette of pale neutrals of period interiors everywhere, rather than the merry chaos of books and bibelots that I like to think of it having in Norah Lofts's day. Houses matter to writers; we relish installing our characters in them; we like them to do well. Norah Lofts trained as a teacher, and began with one book; by the end of her life she had written more than fifty, and was living here. In her Suffolk trilogy, which follows the fortunes of a single dwelling over 600 years, *The Town House* begins as 'two tiny rooms and a kitchen', built in the Abbey's old vineyard, then grows until it is 'two houses, divided by a wide cobbled passage ... big enough and high enough, when it was fully open, to allow a pack pony loaded, to trot in'. By book two, it is so large it reduces onlookers to awe and admiration, and has shining glass in its windows. Twin and I, suitably awed, stood on the other side of Northgate Street and admired. 'That is a big house,' said Twin, who knows about such things. 'Did she build it?'

Norah Lofts was born in 1904; this house was older than that. 'No, she bought it,' said I.

'That is a lot of books,' said Twin.

'It was. Fifty of them.'

'And look,' said Twin. 'What was the stables for the carriages at the end, and now it is a garage, and a flat for a chauffeur.'

A moment's pause, then 'How very Agatha Christie,' we both said, together.

I have no idea if Norah was a walker, but I suspect so. One of her characters, heartsick Oliver Stanton, certainly is. He is a teacher, too, with an interest in an impromptu playhouse, and takes refuge in words, as do so many of us. He describes how he would

> ... walk along arranging the scenes, building up the characters and composing the speeches. I'd invent situations so comic that I laughed as I walked, or so tragic that I almost wept. I never gave a thought to what would happen to these superb plays of mine when they were written, they were enough in themselves, a kind of mental exercise, and the characters were company for me in my lonely walk.

Because when you walk, you head is free, as well as your feet. At the very start of the trilogy, in book one, Martin Reed and his beloved Kate walk from Norwich to Bury, although it almost kills them, simply so that they too can be free, and together and safe. We walk for those reasons too.

The Elizabethan comic actor Will Kempe was in Bury, a stopping-off point on his famous *Nine Days' Wonder* in which he endeavoured to dance his way from London to Norwich (110 miles, or 180 kilometres). He came by way of Sudbury, where he encountered 'a lusty Country lass' who danced a mile with him along the way to Long Melford. 'My merry Maydemarian', Kempe called her, recalling fondly the 'mirth in her eyes', and how she tucked up her petticoat ready to 'thump it on her way.' He gave her a crown (a coin of five shillings) as a reward, and sounds deeply impressed by her fortitude; 'my pace in dancing,' said Kempe, who had trod the boards with Shakespeare, 'is not ordinary.' A brief pause at Clare, then on he danced to Bury, where the crowds that had come to gawp at the entrance of the Lord Chief Justice into the town (very likely Sir John Popham, at this date), abandoned him entirely to gawp at Kempe instead.

Onwards to Moyse's Hall, which began its life in the 1190s, probably as a merchant's house, and has also been a parcel office, a jail, a police station, and a workhouse. You do begin to see what Bury offered Norah Lofts, as a writer: why she would have needed nowhere else. In 1899 Moyse's Hall became a museum, and in the 1970s it was being run by my mother's friend Elizabeth Owles, a tiny spider monkey of a woman with glittering dark eyes and long dark greying hair, wrapped in two thin plaits about her head. And how did my mother come to know her? Because when that stuttering line of light and dark appeared in the side of the irrigation ditch in the field beside our house, my mother – ever the romantic, ever in search of the wondrous, and with an eye to Sutton Hoo just across the River Deben – called Ipswich Museum, and from then on was a volunteer field hand on dig after dig.

Twin and I were walking, not museum-visiting, and we had Hans with us, so we eschewed entering the museum, although if you are following us in real life, you most certainly should not. Its most famous exhibit is the account of the trial of William Corder, for the infamous 'Murder in the

Red Barn' at Polstead in 1827. (The moral of this story is, if you are a village maiden, do not walk out alone at night to meet your untrustworthy lover.) The account of the trial, as I informed Twin (who is a deal more squeamish than I) is meant to have been bound in Corder's own skin after he was hung for young Maria Marten's murder. I very much doubt that the museum any longer allows this to be inspected as I, as a tween, was allowed to inspect it, and I have no idea if the story about it being bound in Corder's skin is true, but as I gleefully described to Twin (who obliged by doing that little dance where you flap your fingers, as if trying to shake yourself free of such appalling details), there was something about the pores in the leather that looked very, very human.

On again, to Bury's nineteenth-century heyday – the Buttermarket and the Corn Exchange, and the part of town where you walk to the purring of cars over cobbles, where cars are allowed at all. The writer Adrian Bell was here while apprenticed to a farmer in nearby Bradfield St George. The apprenticeship took, and Bell farmed in Suffolk all his life, but he also wrote – his first book, *Corduroy*, came out in 1930. In it, Bury is Stambury, 'a fine and ancient town, containing squares of Georgian houses, and churches in the noble Suffolk style. It had its polite street, where on days other than market-days the county gentry shopped.' This was the Buttermarket, where 'beef and pork and poultry were turned by the alchemy of the coin to feminine adornments, tobacco, silks, and scents. Here wives and daughters strolled.' They do so still, although it was something of a surprise to encounter so persistently the smell of skunk (that was never a feature on my school trips), and to see that the Corn Exchange was now a Wetherspoons, and that Sneezums the jewellers, whose windows were such a highlight of school trips, had become a betting shop; but then what were the farmers and merchants who once gathered here on Cornhill doing whilst their wives and daughters strolled, but betting on the weather and their crops? Down Guildhall Street we went, then Westgate Street, a zig and a zag to Hospital Road, and Ouida's birthplace was before us: one half of a paired terrace, with self-effacing plaque fixed to its side wall ('Ouida' being a childish mispronunciation of her middle name, Louise). Bury has a long memory. It has not forgiven this native daughter yet.

Yet for all the scorn Ouida poured upon this 'small, spiteful country town', I think it stayed with her. In *Two Little Wooden Shoes* she has one of her characters (a child) exclaim 'I want to know all about the people who lived before us; I want to know what the stars are, and what the wind is; I want to know where the lark goes when you lose him out of sight against the sun'. And from her adopted home in Italy, she inveighed against the 'guano-dressed, phosphate-dosed, chemically-treated [sic] fields and gardens of the future,' the 'chemicals, poured over vineyards and farm lands.' She thundered her fury at animal cruelty of all kinds, and at the notion that women were not allowed to walk in public on their own, and against cheap factory-made shoes ('the vast mass of the population of every "civilised" nation has deformed feet'). Not all her views were so modern ('To teach the small child to care for flowers ... [is] to lead him also to a taste and feeling which will ... render him thoughtful and sympathetic when he deals with those sensitive plants, – the souls of women.'), but after a life full of success and renown and *wild* extravagance, she didn't deserve to die reliant on the charity of the few friends she had left, and with her only belongings in the local pawnshop. We cannot all be Norah Lofts.

When did women walking become a thing? When did it become more than something we did, which obviously has been the case for millennia, but instead became something we spoke about, and wrote about, and celebrated, and co-opted into our quiver of rights? When did we start claiming routes through the world? Kerri Andrews begins her history of women walking in the mid-eighteenth century with the poet Elizabeth Carter, but that's an awful lot of centuries in which our walking left no track at all, or almost none. My mother's mother brought up nine children and buried three of them, more or less on her own until my grandfather retired from the navy, yet according to my mother, never walked for pleasure or simply to clear her head without making up some little parcel of nothing to carry with her, string looped about one finger, in order to supply a reason for her having left the house. We women have a lot of walking still to do, thought I, as Twin and I turned gratefully away from the traffic on Cullum Road and out across the water meadows.

The moment we did, all the traffic noise fell away and a whole other world opened up to welcome us: one rustling with mighty willow trees, and with bullrushes rising through it as regular as railings, and alive with tiny birds – blue tits, great tits, and a robin that perched to watch us from no more than a foot away – and cascades of birdsong. 'To be buried in Nature is perpetually distracting,' says Frédéric Gros. (You can hear the 'harrumph!') 'Everything talks to you, greets you, demands your attention: trees, flowers, the colour of the roads. The sigh of the wind, the buzzing of insects, the babble of streams, the impact of your feet on the ground: a whole rustling murmur.' Yes, it does, and how glorious is that? In Robert Bloomfield's poem 'The Farmer's Boy', the boy, Giles, heading off into his tasks for the day, is so transported by 'Nature's music' that he starts to sing along with it:

> The blackbird strove with emulation sweet,
> And Echo answer'd from her close retreat;
> The sporting white-throat on some twig's end borne,
> Pour'd hymns to freedom and the rising morn;
> Stopt in her song perchance the starting thrush
> Shook a white shower from the black-thorn bush,
> Where dew-drops thick as early blossoms hung,
> And trembled as the minstrel sweetly sung.

Bloomfield was born in Honington, 8 miles (13 kilometres) from Bury, in 1766 (his brother worked as a shoemaker in

Bury itself), and is one of the peasant-poets, so-called, like John Clare up in Northamptonshire. The yoking together of those two words should alert you to the amazement with which the eighteenth century greeted the notion that those without an independent income or a university degree might by some divine gift have poetry in their souls, as opposed to them simply having done the hard yards of all writers: determination and perseverance and thinking, thinking, thinking. Did Bloomfield walk in these water meadows? Centuries before, was John Lydgate thinking of this place when he wrote of 'a heavenly compline', of the birds' evensong of 'sugared harmony'?

To add to the distractions of the path, other walkers, and other dogs. An unwritten rule: you may nod to the other walkers, but you unfailingly fall into conversation with the dogs, especially if, like Hans, they are so eager to get to know you, too. 'We talk of men keeping dogs,' says Dickens in *The Uncommercial Traveller*, 'but we might often talk more expressively of dogs keeping men.' Meanwhile 30 metres above us, or maybe more (I have no more sense of distance than I have of direction), part but not part of the world beneath, two more birds pirouetted smoothly about each other, the tesselated undersides to their wings briefly gleaming as they flew, finger-feathers playing with the air. Sparrowhawks. Merlin gives a 'Bird of the Day' to aim at spotting; today, this was ours. A good omen. Twin and I backslapped each other to mark it.

Sometimes, if you are lucky (and now I was feeling lucky) walking allows you to slip into that fugue state where time moves along outside of you. Running can do the same. Writing, too – there are days when I have sat down at my desk and looked up to find it growing dark outside, with no sense of time having passed, of anything from the world outside whatsoever. Dickens walked on purpose, I think, to get to this state of almost self-hypnosis. He exhausted his friends on walks around his home at Gad's Hill Place in Kent; in his study he strode between desk and mirror, trying out lines of dialogue, acting out this scene and that, acting his characters, too. He confides in *The Uncommercial Traveller* that 'if I cherished betting propensities, I should probably be found registered in sporting newspapers under some such title as the Elastic Novice, challenging all eleven stone mankind to competition in walking.' Samuel Pepys could read as he walked, but Dickens claimed he could walk as he slept and still be writing, somewhere up in his head:

> Mile after mile I walked, without the slightest sense of exertion, dozing heavily and dreaming constantly. It was only when I made a stumble like a drunken man, or struck out into the road to avoid a horseman close upon me on the path – who had no existence – that I came to myself and looked about ... I sometimes argue with myself that I know I cannot be awake, for, if I were, I should not be half so ready. The readiness is not imaginary, because I often recall long strings of verses, and many turns of fluent speech, after I am broad awake.

I am not that bad, but perhaps this writerly propensity to self-hypnosis, to momentarily leaving the world, is another reason why I like to walk with a companion, to provide the timely nudge back into the here and now. On we went – briefly through a housing estate (but even the housing estates seem of a higher quality in Bury than they might be elsewhere) and onto Hardwick Heath.

Jocelin of Brakelond, who was a sort of company secretary to the Abbey and whose *Chronicle* covers its fortunes from 1173 to 1202, describes Hardwick Heath as the abode of villeins, the lowest of the low, among whose tasks were the emptying of the monastery latrines. Yet it was also home to Hardwick House – demolished in the 1920s, but grand enough in its heyday to have entertained Elizabeth I and as imposing as anything imagined by Norah Lofts. It was also a prisoner-of-war encampment during the Second World War, but it took Twin to point out that the circular pan of concrete I had jokingly identified as a place for practising shotput was in fact a helicopter landing pad, and the two men in green surgical scrubs waiting beside it were no doubt waiting for an air ambulance, so we hurried ourselves along out of their way. Autumn seemed to have arrived in Hardwick Heath earlier than any place else in Bury, the leaves moving with that susurration of autumn dryness, and all its colours overlaid with a dusting of bronze. Here was Hencote Lane. Here was Nowton Road. A staggered crossing over a dual carriageway, with the din of the A14 growing unpleasantly louder in the distance, and here was the River Lark, one of England's chalk streams. There are only 300 such worldwide, fed by springs in chalk bedrock; England has almost all of them.

The Lark was just visible through the usual lattice of leaves and bramble, its water reflective as a mirror – one sign of a chalk stream being its absolute clarity. There were no water voles, such as I have seen on a chalk stream in Salisbury running along on top of the mats of crowfoot as if over the deck of a ship, but there was an egret. A white egret, with its wispy crest and that black grape-scissor of a bill, and its tight, tear-shaped body that even here in Suffolk still looked so Egyptian, as if it should be stalking between papyrus on the wall of a tomb rather than hiding away behind the nettles and hawthorns – hawthorns so heavily and vibrantly berried they looked as if they had been caught in spray after spray of blood. If the heaviness of the berry crop is the weather-indicator that folklore would have it be, this coming winter was going to be a beast. Then, as we turned back toward Bury and the Abbey Gardens, we were greeted by a gangling alder tree, a juvenile, decked with ribbons of yellow and blue, planted to commemorate all those who had fallen in Ukraine's war against its invader. It would grow taller, and sturdier, and it would live a long, long time: nothing stops an alder. Conditions that would rot another tree where it stands only makes alder wood stronger and harder. Good choice.

Bury has a very elegant cathedral. Thanks to Henry VIII (and after him, that Puritan wrecking ball William Dowsing), it has the ruins of the old abbey to make it picturesque, but the Cathedral (St James's Church, as was) has virtues of its own. It is very co-ordinated, to begin with, in a manner that the visual cortex finds deeply satisfying. Outside, one pinnacle is echoed by another; within, each arch and curve has its pair. John Wastell, the master mason responsible for much of what the visitor sees today, also worked on King's College in Cambridge, another masterpiece in the Perpendicular style, and by the time they got to the Perpendicular in the evolution of such spaces, the master masons of the 1500s knew what they were doing. It is also dog-friendly, bless it, although

Hans, having hoovered his complimentary dog biscuit from the floor, took exception to the speaker addressing the conference taking place within the nave of the Cathedral and we had to exit rather sooner than planned. It is quite stupendous, the echoes you can generate from a foot off the floor in a vaulted space with a few good countertenor yips. In any case, you will be unsurprised to learn I wanted to investigate the churchyard, especially the charnel house, which was only rediscovered in 1845 when some poor walker is meant to have fallen into it as the ground gave way beneath him. I am not quite sure I believe that – the charnel house looks to sit proud of the ground around it to me, and is now well railed off – but what stories wait behind those railings. Mary Haselton, killed by a flash of lightning at the age of nine, 'being in the Act of Prayer.' Captain Bartholomew Gosnold, who died in Jamestown, Virginia in 1607, far from his wife Mary, who was buried here in 1665, and his little daughter Martha, who had died in 1598. But he took her with him. He named Martha's Vineyard, Massachusetts, in her honour.

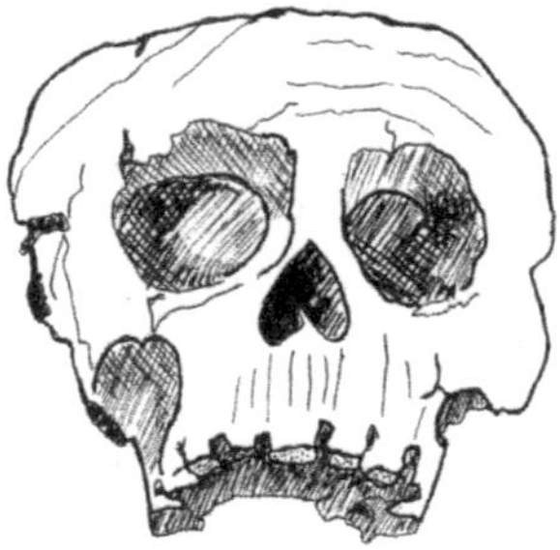

Adrian Bell came here too:

> At the end of the town ... were the ruins of a great abbey, a memory of old ecclesiastical significance. Public gardens had been laid out within the walls. They were deserted to-day. I walked the lawns under bare boughs tranced to the stillness of stone in the frosty air. Shattered arches stood up lonely from the grass. A door stood open in an enclosure of ruined wall. I looked in, and found a gardener there sweeping up the last leaves. It had been a family burial place, he said. 'The mossy leum, they call it.' He looked around. 'There ain't much moss here now, but doubtless there was at one time.'

Bell's first shy admission that he wanted to write (which happened on a walk with his father, I would have you note), was greeted with the response that 'the desire to write in the young was but a manifestation of the sexual impulse. This,' said Bell, 'had confirmed my worst fears – that there was nothing "in me" after all ... So I had bowed to his implication that my dreams and visitations were one with the spots on my face, and only pleaded that my life should be something in the open air.' He got his wish. But you cannot stop a writer writing. 'He is up at his loom,' says Robert Louis Stevenson, 'weaving and weaving, to set the landscape to words.' Most poignant of all the epitaphs in the charnel house is that to Henry Cockton, 'Author of "Valentine Vox", "Sylvester

Sound", "The Love Match", and other works.' Cockton married a local girl, daughter of the landlady of The Seven Stars in Long Brackland. He has a plaque there, like Ouida. He strove all his life to be Dickens and wrote novel after novel featuring good-hearted bumblers such as himself, but while they all found fame and fortune, Henry did not. 'Why do I bother to describe it?' Stella asks at the end of *The Brimstone Wedding*, and of her life. 'What does it matter now?' Because you are a writer, that's why, and the bug in your head gives you no peace unless you are weaving those words out of the air. Lydgate wrote 150,000 rhyming couplets in his life; I think the last word goes to him, from his 'Kalendare'.

> So may we dance with holy Saint Giles,
> In heaven on high after this little while.

Amen to that.

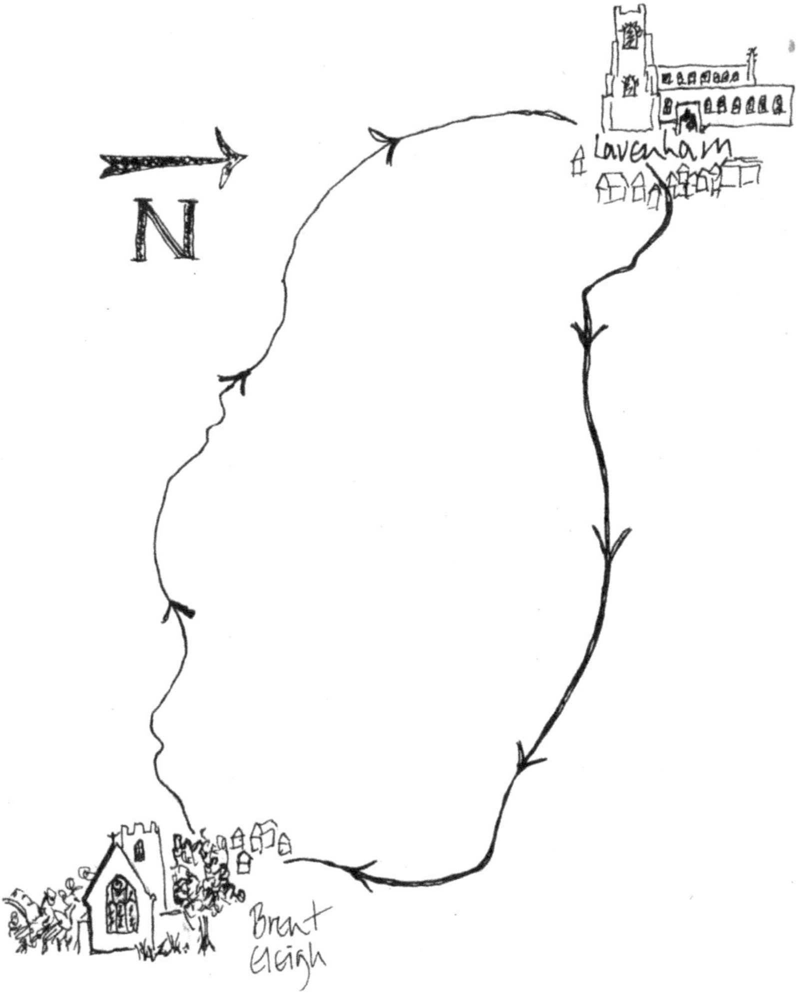
N
Lavenham
Brent
Eleigh

2

Into the Green

Lavenham

It is humbling, as a writer, to dig about in the thoughts of other writers – not because what you discover feels so familiar (although it does), but because so many of the writers you encounter have dropped so much further out of sight than they surely would ever have thought possible. Who, for example, aside from students with a reading list, reads Ouida now? We know Defoe, but who remembers John Kirby and his *Suffolk Traveller* of 1764, with its descriptions of the smallest individual parish and its twenty pages of carefully measured routes from here to there – because that was how you did it, or hoped to do it, in the days before we had GPS and plant- and bird-recognition software and all our correspondence and conversations and every like or dislike as well as every penny to our name all on one wee handheld thing:

> From the Swan-Inn [Lavenham] turn on the Left at the Corner of the Houfe; at the End of the Street the forward Road to Kettlebaston, turn on the Right; at 7 f[urlongs], cross Brent Ely first Bridge ...

says Kirby, giving his own version of a walk into the green. Or William Alfred Dutt himself, 'noted' as a recluse, as his biography describes him (although surely if you have made yourself noted as a recluse, you are doing it wrong), and who lived in a cottage full of books in the high north of Suffolk, on the coast at Carlton Colville. A cottage full of books on the coast – how heavenly would that be, let alone to live in it as a flesh-and-blood oxymoron. Dutt published his *Literary Associations* in 1907, which was how I first came across him, lying in an apple crate in a second-hand bookshop. J. E. Vincent was loud in his praise of Dutt in his own *Through East Anglia in a Motor Car*: 'a careful and fascinating writer, equally learned in antiquities and in ornithology, and very much at home in East Anglia.' For the *rambleuse* Dutt's *Literary Associations* are a cookie jar, with its snippets on Dickens and Bloomfield and FitzGerald and Suffolk's other great poet George Crabbe, but who would go to Dutt to discover more of any of these now? Or there is the journalist Clement King Shorter who, again in 1907, published his *Immortal Memories* – a collection of addresses given, so he tells us, 'at the request of various literary societies and commemorative committees', including one given in 1901 also entitled 'Literary Associations of East Anglia', at a dinner given in honour of one William Alfred Dutt. But neither this, nor Dutt's own book, have brought much in the way of immortality to either man, nor to J. E. Vincent – although his fruity, petrol-head prose still has great charm, at least to me. Even (much more recently) Hammond Innes, who lived out in the green in the village of Kersey and wrote more than thirty best-selling thrillers there – including *The Wreck of the Mary Deare*, which in 1959 became a movie starring Gary Cooper and Charlton Heston, with a supporting cast including Sir Michael Redgrave and Richard Harris and a script by Eric Ambler (seriously, could a writer ask for more?) – even he has titles out of print, including his heartfelt celebration of and thank-you note to the region, *Hammond Innes' East Anglia*. It was published as recently as 1986. The apple crate in the second-hand bookshop is the fate of us all, and probably faster than we would think possible.

From literary obscurity to losing one's way. This must have been so much more frequent an experience than it is today. If you ventured off Suffolk's turnpike roads, if you went deep in the green, a guide such as Kirby's might be all that stood between you and a night sleeping out in the fields. In 1698 Celia Fiennes, that doughty traveller and contemporary of Daniel Defoe, found that her way had gone awry somewhere near Battisford, which is near Battisford Tye, which is near Stowmarket. The business of location, deep in the green, is still cumulative – it's near here, which is near to there (slightly larger), which is near to there (larger yet). The roads don't have alphanumerics, they have names: not B1125, but 'Dark Lane', 'Hall Road', or even (my favourite, and my italics) in many a Suffolk village, '*The* Street'. Says Celia:

> Generally ye people here are able to give so bad a Direction that passengers are at a loss what aime to take: they know scarce 3 mile from their home, and meete them where you will and Enquire how farre to such a place they mind not where they are then, but tell you so farre, wch is the distance from their own houses to yt place.

'Blessed be the villages; that proclaim their titles,' declared J. E. Vincent, with an eye on his fuel-gauge, 'even by modest boards on the post-offices ... for by such boards is the traveller saved from the scorn poured upon him who asks of the rustic the name of his native village'.

The rustics might give so bad a direction, but they might be doing so on purpose. Another of my pet Suffolk writers is Francis Hindes Groome, who was born in Monk Soham (near Framlingham, near Woodbridge) in 1851, and as a young man abandoned an Oxford degree to follow his passion for Romani language and lore and ways of living all over Europe. He gained a Roma honorific as the 'Tarno Rye' (very roughly, the 'young gentleman') and married a Roma woman too (her name has come down to us as Esmerelda

Locke). All this from the son of a Suffolk archdeacon. Before his all-too-early death at the age of fifty, Francis had written half a dozen works on the Roma and edited more, and he also wrote the fondest reminiscence of his father the archdeacon and his friendship with Edward FitzGerald, in which the son's memories and his father's own 'Suffolk stories' grow around each other like woodbine. They include this:

> There was [an] actual balloon, which had gone up somewhere in the West of England, and which came down in (I think) the neighbouring parish of Bedfield. As it floated over Monk Soham, the aeronaut shouted, 'Where am I?' to some harvesters, who, standing in a row, their forefingers pointed at him, shouted back, 'Yeou're in a ballune, bor.'

Like I said, the Suffolk sense of humour. Do not underestimate it.

Monk Soham, viewed from above, has more field path than road. Its sister village, Earl Soham, is larger and nearer to Framlingham. Framlingham counts as a town, in that it has a market and a castle, but as Dutt points out, 'Suffolk is a county of small towns which are little more than villages,' and the distinction between the two is a bit woo-wah, as we say where I come from. The two Sohams, for example, were once as one. Monk Soham had monks and their fishponds, and even in 1086, a church; Earl Soham had the Bigods, earls of Norfolk, who also owned Framlingham Castle. One now has but a single road, curving cautiously about it, and a population of some 150 souls; the other was measured along with that of Charsfield in 2011 as having over 2,000. Charsfield is one among the portmanteau of actual villages to be found hiding within Ronald Blythe's ur-village of *Akenfield*; but Earl Soham has its own claim to fame – between 1964 and 1967, the novelist Patricia Highsmith lived there, in Bridge Cottage, on (of course) The Street.

A love affair had brought Highsmith to England, a love affair with a married woman. The pair trysted first in Aldeburgh, where 'C' or 'Caroline' as she has become known, may have already owned a cottage (there is still something of a mystery over who among Highsmith's many lovers this woman was), then Highsmith bought Bridge Cottage as a – what? A love nest, deep in the green? A place where the endlessly peripatetic writer might draw breath? The love affair, at least on Highsmith's side, was more intense and, when bad, more intensely unhappy than any she had known before ('smitten and smashed' was how she would describe it in her diary), and even its highpoints have that febrile fragility to them, where one of those involved feels they hardly dare utter a word for fear of ruining everything. 'I am absolutely sick for her,' she wrote, 'and I must summon up every bit of determination and courage that I possess in order to carry on alone.' God knows Highsmith was capable of putting herself first in most situations, and had to a nicety that writerly trick in the midst of domestic trauma of standing apart from herself and taking notes, but she wasn't without heart, or conscience, or sense. In her misery, as her real life unravelled beyond her control, who among the writerly community in Suffolk did she turn to for solace? Ronald Blythe.

Blythe, who was also gay, thought that Highsmith was simply in search of comfort. It sounds as if they got into bed together out of not much more than curiosity, then found themselves aroused enough to attempt to have sex. Highsmith described straight sex as being 'raped in the wrong place' (try as I might, I cannot parse that one out), but then she also likened the experience of falling in love to being 'shot in the face', while Blythe reflected with typical generosity that 'one did sometimes feel as if one was subject matter'. I hope the present inhabitants of Bridge Cottage have the happiest and most fulfilled of private lives, but in the mid-1960s that roof must have covered some of the worst bad sex in history. The great affair with 'C', after all that, ended in a final childish tantrum on C's part and a flouncing out, and Highsmith's departure from England altogether. But it, or Suffolk, also saw the creation of *A Suspension of Mercy*, published in 1965: Highsmith at her most compulsively creepy. True, there are strange anachronisms ('start the tea-water' for 'put the kettle on') and odd-sounding meals (an invitation to coffee and strawberries in the middle of the afternoon, anyone?), but if you want the scrappy and peculiar interior life of a writer laid bare, this is it.

The engine behind the plot is a pair of houses, built close by each other in an otherwise houseless stretch of Suffolk countryside, in one of which lives Sydney Bartleby, a writer in need of inspiration. His wife Alicia is fed up with him; he is fed up with himself. Life in the Suffolk countryside is solitary, inconvenient and dull. 'Is misery a little bit different when set down on paper?' Highsmith had asked herself, in her diary, and answered 'Yes'.

> He took aimless walks along roads, always wanting to find some woods, to walk into the fields; yet he found no woods, and the fields, deserted as they were, looked to him as if they belonged to some watchful farmer who would ask his business if he set foot in them. Well, what was his business? Nothing. That would sound more suspicious than anything, Sydney supposed. Better to have an answer like, 'I'm interested in rabbits and I thought I saw one disappear down a hole here.' He finally did venture into a few fields, but was never challenged. He would walk for miles, slowly, not thinking of food until he became hungry, which was always after 2.30 p.m., when the pubs were closed and he could get nothing.

Ah, the years when pubs closed their doors after lunch, and every shop was locked for early closing on a Wednesday afternoon. How long ago they seem.

But then, inspiration comes to Sydney in the character of

'the Whip', a criminal mastermind devoid of conventional morality: an alternate persona for Sydney to escape into, just as the character of Ripley had been for Sydney's creator. In his new world of words, Sydney hardly seems to notice when Alicia leaves him, but in her absence, and in character as 'the Whip', he fantasises about how difficult it might be to get rid of an actual body by rolling up an old carpet, driving out into the countryside, and burying it. (Trust me, no writer would find this crackpot behaviour strange in the least. In *Unnatural Causes*, one of her Dalgliesh thrillers with a Suffolk setting, P. D. James has one character explain of another that 'Maurice ... would have walked into hell in the service of his writing.' Yes, we would.) But Sydney's suspicious behaviour is of course spotted by his only neighbour. The police become involved, especially when his wife's whereabouts continue unknown. Sydney's masquerade of guilt – basically to see what it might *feel* like to be guilty of murder – comes closer and closer to getting him arrested for real. At the same time, as Highsmith was herself during her Suffolk moment, he is frustrated by his writing partner; contracts that should be done deals turn out to be no such thing and he has come to despise the novel he is meant to be working on. It's more than a bit meta, is *Suspension of Mercy*, as writers writing about writers cannot help but be. 'Art – working', says Highsmith 'does the same thing as alcohol. It changes the world until it is tolerable.' And where does the idea for 'the Whip' come to Sydney? Of course, on a walk.

Writers mine their own lives all the time. We call this research. '... they're monstrous egotists. Self-confidence, self-examination, self-hatred even ... but it's all about self,' says Susan Ryeland, the editor/investigator in Anthony Horowitz's *Moonflower Murders*, sat in the bar of Branlow Hall, the fictional hotel that fictionally exists near to the very real town of Framlingham. 'A precise, self-opinionated nervous little man, perpetually fretting about his sales, his publicity or his book jackets,' says publisher Max Gurney in *Unnatural Causes*, describing the murder victim whose body has just washed up on a Suffolk beach. 'A typical writer in fact,' responds Dalgliesh.

We also mine the lives of those about us, and call this research too. When not attempting intercourse, Highsmith and Blythe toured the Suffolk churches; recollections of a day spent doing the same stirs in Highsmith's character of Sydney a rare bittersweet memory of his marriage:

> Sydney looked at a brass rubbing he had made of Sir Robert de Bures' mailed feet crossed upon a small worried lion. It was from the church in Acton. He and Alicia had been together that day, very much together, picnicking in the car because it had started to rain, coming home, making love, trimming and matting the brass-rubbing on purple velvet ready for the framer. They had also visited Lavenham and Long Melford churches, Alicia making sketches, Sydney scribbling notes that he thought he might use some time. He had even scribbled a poem ...

The mention of Acton is a Highsmith grace note – Blythe was born there. It is about as deep in the green as you can get. Sir Robert de Bures was buried in Acton All Saints in 1331, and his brass (one of the oldest and finest in existence) shows him in his Crusader kit of chainmail and surcoat, and the lion on which he seems to be balancing does indeed look perturbed at the weight on its back. The real world pokes through. Let us walk. No, let us get ourselves lost.

*

Wool is what this part of Suffolk is all about – churches and wool, and the ways that were the ways before there were tarmacked roads, and the folk who walked them. But let's begin in Lavenham, like John Kirby, with the wool. It built the town; at the turn of the 1500s, when Lavenham was wealthy enough to be paying more taxes than York, it built Lavenham's incongruously huge and lovely church (with a little help from Thomas Spring, known locally as 'Thomas the Rich'). 'Lavenham Blue' broadcloth is what the town was famous for, dyed with woad, or *Isatis tinctoria*, a straggling, yellow-headed runaway of a plant, but one that gives a dye as blue as a bluebell. The whole of Lavenham was one giant woollen mill in its late medieval heyday: the villages on its outskirts carded and spun the wool; the River Brett ran in a culvert under the houses of Water Street to help with the fulling (the shrinking and thickening) of the cloth;

the Wool Hall (now the Swan inn) and the Guild Hall were where the cloth was sold, the industry regulated, and the mighty profits made; the higgledy-piggledy rows of timbered cottages (a-lean like so many houses of cards and timbered because stone as a building material was so much more costly and in Suffolk so scarce) were where the weavers and dyers and fullers lived and worked. Before we get sentimental, you could also view Lavenham as an English medieval version of the Chinese factory towns of today. And wool is the reason we have Lavenham still, when in due course the industry and the markets all moved elsewhere, leaving Lavenham beached at the high-water mark of its medieval fortunes. All that half-timbering, especially when tide-washed to the silver-grey it has on the Guild Hall, could be seen as no more than flotsam.

But oh, what glorious flotsam. How we love our oak-beamed, half-timbered houses with their mustard or rose or terracotta wash, their projecting upper storeys with the warning sign (inevitably dented) marked 'OVERHANGING BUILDING', their cicatrice plaster-pargeting of scrolls and Tudor roses. (Although not all of that is as it might appear: my mother had an old plaster lion's head put up above the door of her antique shop, and was delighted to overhear a man point it out to his wife as having been there 'for centuries'.) 'Over the narrow streets,' writes Dutt in nostalgic reverie (he is talking about Framlingham but the description serves at least as well here),

> … the upper storeys of old, half-timbered houses bend as though seeking support, after centuries of top-heaviness, against the walls across the way; on the plastered shop fronts, on the brackets of the projecting latticed windows, and in the spandrels of old doorways leading into panelled halls and stone-paved courts, there are curious heraldic carvings reminding one of lords and abbots of feudal times …

Lavenham is a Suffolk straight out of central casting – the perfect bucolic Suffolk town, half-timbered, pink-washed, with all the virtues we ascribe our forefathers and none of their hardships. (It is no surprise at all to discover in this faery-land of Englishness that 'Twinkle, Twinkle, Little Star' was written here by one Jane Taylor, in Shilling Street.) 'Oak is such a wonderful wood,' Hammond Innes writes, thumping his chest. 'The texture of it, that close, slow-grown grain … It is such a virile wood. It planes and chisels so robustly, yet with an almost silky texture when carefully smoothed. It is a very sensuous wood. Every carpenter loves it.' To him, walking through Lavenham was like 'walking through a petrified forest where every tree has been fashioned by man.'

Perhaps part of why we love half-timbering is because it shows its workings. Its outside speaks of its inside: low ceilings; wide-planked floors; tiny-paned windows; inglenook fireplaces; four-poster beds. It speaks, quietly but firmly, of trustworthy traditions, simpler times (or so we picture them);

of having lasted centuries, sheltered generations; it murmurs to the imagination *I will shelter you too*. It is anthropomorphic architecture: it slouches, sticks its elbows out, tilts its head to peer down at you. My mother, I am sure, believed in her heart of hearts that if she could only live in a place with beams, it would make her everything she wanted to be. She would wake within it like the princess, with every single hard and inconvenient pea removed from her life. It is, I think, a dream shared by many, hence that fact that today, a half-timbered house speaks of a fully buttressed income.

Twin and I began this walk in Lavenham's marketplace, with its Market Cross behind us, topped with a spike that looks as if it has been the target of bolts of Suffolk lightning since the days of Thomas the Rich at least. Little Hall (late fourteenth century), and the Great House (Georgian frontage) were to our right, and the Angel Hotel, as was, to our left. Prentice Street was in front. We descended, making the best peace we could with the fact that like my mother, we were unable to pass a single 'For Sale' board without lusting after the house on which it was displayed. The bottom of Prentice Street is Lower Road. Here, as it has done for centuries, Lavenham comes to a halt.

Lower Road is one of those optimistic Suffolk streets where a thin white line, painted three inches away from the verge, is to be taken as making the road entirely safe for pedestrians, something like the protective chalk circle used by those attempting to summon Lucifer, and we all know how that works out. Thankfully, Lower Road had no traffic on it whatsoever, and no noise but the whispering of the wind in the trees above us – 'the winds that sets the trees a-talking' as Stevenson puts it – and the thrashings about of some of the largest, fattest wood pigeons I have ever seen, flailing around in the branches as they tried to keep their balance. Lower Road ultimately leads back into Lavenham again, but before it could do so, to the left there was an almost unnoticeable bridge over the River Brett.

It would be delightful to report that the Brett was faintly tinged with bluebell blue after all those centuries of running under the woad-stained culverts of Water Street, but it was not. In fact, even after all the sudden summer rains, it was no more than a blur of darker green vegetation over a line of mud. But to one side of the bridge a summer storm had overthrown an enormous white willow, with a violence that made me suspect not so much the wind as one of those same bolts of Suffolk lightning. Ever since the days of Aesop's *Fables*, willows famously bend with the wind when the oak refuses; this one, however, had not only fallen but seemed to have wrenched itself over in its fall, and recently too. The broken trunk was nothing but splinters and spillikins pointing at the sky, although its leaves were streaming in the breeze as if still on the crown of the tree, oblivious to the nettles and foxgloves now growing through them. It can be mighty hard to kill a tree.

Across the bridge was Clay Lane, and plenty clay-ey it was,

too. This grey-brown earth – summer hard, baked rigid – is I bet to be found in the daub overlaying the willow-wattle, the wooden lattice used to infill between the oak timbers of many of Lavenham's houses. Oak, willow, clay, add water – in Suffolk, that means you have a house. Walk across the top of Clay Hill and you could start to fill its pantry – there were wild-grown apples, rosehips, blackberries and sloes, although many of the blackberries, to my regret, were past their best; their drupelets, the little black beads, already had that spoiled and shrivelled look to them. According to legend, this is the result of them having been spat on by the Devil (and who wants to find themselves eating devil spit?), but, according to the same legend, that is not meant to happen until after Michaelmas (29 September, or old-style, 10 October). There, the Georgian calendar brought the date for no more blackberries forward by eleven days; now global warming has apparently brought it forward by a month or more. The sloes, however, were perfection – blushed with the true sloe violet bloom, fat and round, and so good a crop it was as if they were bubbling along the branches of the bushes. I seized one of Hans's unused poo-bags and set to harvesting, explaining to Twin the makings and the cheering effects, let us call them, in the depths of winter, of sloe gin.

More people should make sloe gin. All you need is quantity of sloes, half their weight in sugar, and a litre of good gin per kilo of berries (Adnams is perfect). Wash the sloes to get the dust of the fields off them, pat them dry, then prick them all over with a cocktail stick or silver pin, or put them in the freezer to mimic the workings of the first frost in rupturing their violet skins. The point is to get the garnet juices to run into the gin. Mix everything together in a good big jar. Shake it up. Put it away in the dark. Every week, give it another shake and put it away again. In two months' time, you will have an innocent-looking, fiendishly strong, beautifully fragrant, raspberry-pink liqueur, to sip in your favourite chair whilst enjoying a good book. What are you waiting for?

An insane twiddle at the highest pitch the human ear can catch moved along the interior of the hedges with us as we walked – a Goldcrest, said Merlin, putting a dot on the map, adding 'It looks like you saw the bird here'. Only of course I hadn't seen it, I had only heard it, and for the second time, the first being in Wales. 'I do not have a Goldcrest,' said Twin, bringing out her phone, at which point of course the Goldcrest fell silent, so I showed her on mine – this tiny, furious-looking thing, with its bright yellow Travis Bickle mohican. 'I do not have one,' Twin said again. It's dreadful, quite how competitive Merlin can make you, but then twitchers have been cut-throat since birdwatching began.

Behind us, the furrows stretched back to a vanishing point. The furrows of a ploughed field, let alone one ploughed through Suffolk clay – does anything speak of solitary labour more loudly than that? There's a place in *The Farmer's Boy* where Giles goes ploughing:

> ... when Giles with wearying strides
> From ridge to ridge the ponderous harrow guides;
> His heels deep sinking every step he goes,
> Till dirt usurp the empire of his shoes.
> Welcome green headland! firm beneath his feet;
> Welcome the friendly bank's refreshing seat

This is made even more poignant if you know that Robert Bloomfield was so fragile a being he only reached five feet (just over 1.5 metres) tall as a full-grown man. I've hauled my deep-sinking heels over those furrows too – along with volunteering herself to Elizabeth Owles, my mother volunteered me too. Children, close to the ground and with sharp eyes, are excellent field-walkers, and my mother was convinced we would find a torc, or a leather bag of silver Saxon coins at least, waiting for us to pass by. Both have been found in Suffolk – in fact, courtesy of Elizabeth Owles, I have held an Iron Age gold torc, one of the Belstead hoard. Touching it made my fingertips fizz. But if there was another out there waiting for me to discover it, it is waiting still. I found flints – 'faery shot', the worked flints of our ancestors used to be known as – and shards of shiny Samian pottery and even the verdigris of Roman bronze, but oh how I hated the clay, and lifting my tired legs over one furrow after the other until the bank was gained again. Now, with my head in the space of this book for over a year, I couldn't look at the field without thinking of Adrian Bell's many descriptions of ploughing with horses, of learning to 'bear on the plough', when to narrow the furrow, when to widen it, of watching to keep the lines straight ...

> As I stood preparing to voyage across the field once more I made my plans. In the middle I must shave a narrower furrow to straighten the kink, and farther on a wider one to rectify the bulge. But it was impossible to see when one was at the right spot for the variation, and on reaching the end of the stretch I found sometimes that I had made another kink and another bulge.

Keep the lines straight. Expand here, cut there ... You can see where I am going with this. At the end of all this hard labour,

Bell allows himself to reflect for a moment on all the other ways of earning a living, and the 'rat-like scurryings', as he puts it, into the London Underground with which he might otherwise have been starting and ending his day. Quite. Writing may be solitary, it may sometimes feel as if you are pulling a plough uphill through mud, or even molten lava, but it is not that. Or, as one of Bell's neighbours commented of another, a civil servant: 'Bless you, he don't do no work; he just sit a-writing all day!'

On we went, me pondering out loud all the ways in which tech has transformed the business of taking a walk. As a teenager walking our wolfhound, Fergus, around the village where I grew up, I had maybe half a dozen field paths as dog-walking routes, and only the haziest idea how any of them connected with any other, or where, beyond the village, they might lead. Now I tap a screen and I can locate myself, construct a route at will, share it with whomever I wish, inventorise its birdlife, and identify its plants. Before all that was even dreamed of, who walked here? Before there were cars on the road, you used the road, so who made and used these paths? We were walking through real, tangled, unmonitored woodland, where fallen branches had rotted where they fell, and Old Man's Beard, *Clematis vitalba*, had strung itself from tree to tree on stems as thick as hawsers. So who kept this path open, and why? Farm workers, gamekeepers, poachers, highwaymen? 'Poachers and highwaymen,' said Twin, without hesitation. Hans, meanwhile, was receiving his own version of text messages, delivered straight to the liquorice ferrule of his nose every couple of inches or so – a reminder of yet another of the secret worlds that exist about us; not just the birdlife but the rabbits, badgers, foxes, beetles, other dogs ... there was a thought emerging into visibility for me, the way some feature on the horizon gradually assumes a form as you walk toward it. This one was shaped not just by the autonomy of walking, but by a new, on-the-ground comprehension of the significance of it as an action with an aim, a destination: a claiming of the land as a literal means to an end, of imposing upon it direction, intent. Ownership. Somewhere within the lanes around Lavenham, perhaps even those Twin and I and Hans were making our way along, are the boundaries of the parish, and as George Ewart Evans describes in *The Pattern Under the Plough*, boundaries were there to be watched over, maintained where they should be, with no encroachments, neither yours nor your neighbours. He traces the age-old ceremony of beating the bounds back to two Roman festivals, one of them the Ambarvalia, a joyful processing around the newly ploughed fields in spring, on land that had been rendered doubly submissive, first claimed and then farmed. We certainly had Romans here in Suffolk, alternately fleeing or hunting the native Iceni and Trinovantes, dropping the bronze pins from their cloaks as they did so, but surely this impulse to walk the edges of what is yours must go back long beyond. This was what we had all done, throughout the ages: we walked from there to here, and then when we settled, we walked not in a line but in a circle, around what we claimed as ours. Somewhere in all our histories there is a bloody long walk. I shared this brilliance with Twin. 'Not mine,' Twin replied, and proceeded to explain how her ancestors, the Schwepckes, were from the lazy Swabians, who stayed where they were. The enterprising Swabians kept on going, right down to Stuttgart. Her father had joined the German navy in the Second World War because he disliked walking so much, and there is not a lot of marching in the navy. 'I am a complete abnormality where my family is concerned,' said Twin, striding along, as Hans came hurtling down the path to catch us up, his tail like an ostrich feather, albeit one a deal less snowy than it had been when we set off.

*

The goal of this walk was the village of Brent Eleigh – one of those same villages where the wool was spun to go to Lavenham's weavers. To be specific, it wasn't the village itself, but Brent Eleigh's church, St Mary's, and the wall paintings inside, which quite incredibly are so old that had Sir Robert de Bures ever come here, he might have admired them too. The sense of this part of Suffolk being untouched and unchanging made it a favourite cycle-ride for Ronald Blythe:

> The land is all view and I am all viewer, and soon the ecological patterns and colours not only spread before me but permeate me, and I become part of what I am

seeing. I can see patches of medieval forest here and there among the corn, and although I know that 'the woods decay and fall', I also know that in comparison with human flesh they take ages to do so. Thus its ancientness must be one of the healing factors of landscape.

As with Earl and Monk Soham, Brent Eleigh also has a twin, Monks Eleigh, so named after it was given to the monks of the See of Canterbury. Monks Eleigh is the bigger, with a population of over 500; Brent Eleigh doesn't reach a third of that. Sebald talks of Suffolk villages whose souls number no more than they did in the Middle Ages, and you have to wonder at what it can have been like if you were to arrive in one of these villages, deep in the green, in the 1300s, from a metropolis such as Canterbury with its thousands of pilgrims and hundreds of miracles, its stained glass and the great golden shrine of Thomas Beckett; with its learning and scriptorium and its international community, to be here among those who knew 'scarce three miles from their home'? But each such community had its church and congregation, nonetheless, and 400 years later, in his 1643 rampage through East Anglia, William Dowsing was determined to find them all. 'At Haverhill,' (20 miles, or 30 kilometres, west of Brent Eleigh) he recorded gleefully in his *Journal*, 'we brake down about a hundred superstitious pictures [he means the church's stained-glass windows] and 7 fryers hugging a nun.' At Stowmarket (12 miles, or 20 kilometres, north-east of Brent Eleigh) 'We gave order to break down 70 superstitious pictures and to level the chancel.' Lord, what we lost. Going about the country 'like a Bedlam' was one description of Dowsing. He certainly did.

The path rounded a curve. Ahead of us were two men: one younger, armed with a hedge trimmer, actively chopping and clearing, and one older, stood to the side, supervising watchfully, hands clasped in immemorial manner over a shepherd's crook. It was a very fine crook. It looked as if head, heal, and shank were as they had grown, cut from the parent tree as one. It caught my eye.

We paused. We exchanged greetings. Writers are allowed to do more than that, they are allowed to be shamelessly nosy. What were these two doing, clearing the path, and why? 'For the pheasants,' came the at first surprising reply. I know pheasants are maybe the stupidest birds who ever grew a feather, but surely they could make paths of their own? What was meant of course was not the birds, but those shooting them. The local syndicate was paying to keep these paths open. 'But that is still the land being cared for,' said Twin, reasonably enough, as we walked on. 'Curated,' said I.

I kept thinking of the older man's crook. There is a passage in *Akenfield* where one of Blythe's villagers talks of his father, a wheelwright, going to the hedges for a different sort of harvest:

> He'd walk through the lanes and note the ashes and when he saw a good one, he'd buy it, cut it down and let it lie in

> the ditch for a couple of years until the bark fell off. Then it was ready. He also looked for shaft wood. If you look at the ash trees you'll find that many of their boughs grow in the shape of shafts. When my father saw a good shaft shape a-growing, he'd keep his eye on it until it was just the right size to cut and plane. Then he'd have it.

Which would be a whole other way of reading the landscape, if one only had the expertise required to do it. Mine extended to peering at my phone yet again at the re-appearance of tarmacked road ahead of us, at the end of the track. There was a signpost, just about poking its head over the high-grown, end-of-summer grasses. 'Hall Road,' said I. 'Brent Eleigh half a mile. We turn here.'

*

Brent Eleigh Hall, or rather its gates and gatehouse, is the first thing you see on entering the village by Hall Road. The gates are of the type that might have a Miss Haversham living behind them, piebald with grey and yellow lichen, standing a little open, one finial furry with moss. The hall, apparently, has a most unusual front, but although I pondered walking up the drive and announcing, like Sydney Bartleby and his rabbits, 'Good morning. I have an interest in giant Tuscan porticos,' I decided against it. The gatehouse also presents a bold gable to the road, on which there is a heraldic crest proudly announcing *Je trouve bien* – 'I find well' is the literal translation, but I suspect 'I find good' is closer to the spirit intended. I hoped that we would do so too. Having walked Twin and Hans out here, I was by no means sure the church would be open – its famous wall painting was horribly defaced by a latter-day Dowsing in 2016 and took months of punctilious care to restore. There is always some utter waste of skin, either incapable of comprehending what they're looking at or so wholly intimidated by it that they decide no-one else should see it either – it's the history of iconoclasm the world over. But those who look after Brent Eleigh Church are clearly more generous and optimistic in their view of human nature than me. A cheery notice informed us the church would welcome us (another, inside, begged us to forgive the plastic covering the altar itself, but 'we have not yet managed to church-train our bats'); we walked through the little churchyard, under the trees, and there it was, square towered, flint walled, with flagstone floor and with that churchy quiet inside that, as Ruth Rendell put it, 'slips over you', and the green of the trees outside filling the church with a mermaid-y light. There were box pews, whose survival alone would be wonder enough (more beating or preservation of the bounds, but in this case between those of different social classes within the congregation). There were well-worn slabs of dark granite let into the floor, since we speak of worlds invisible: *ARTUTI CLARK, RECTORIS*. His wife. His son, another Arthur. A collection of little Snapes

– Alicia, Richard Miles, Frederic Agar, John Peers. At seventeen, Alicia was by far the oldest. A ridiculously ostentatious memorial (for a tiny Suffolk church) to an Edward Colman, which sits him behind spiked iron railings like some animal of uncertain temperament in an old-fashioned zoo, yet which is redeemed by having him lounge, propped up on his elbow, with his other hand held out as if asking through the railings for a peanut. Close by, a memorial to one Mary Goate:

> She died on the 17th Feb, 1804, having attain'd the great age of 95, and might have been accounted a rare instance of happy longevity, but that in the last year of her life She had the misfortune to survive her tenderly affectionate youngest daughter and her only and best of Sons, which brought her with sorrow to the grave.

What poetry some of these old memorials attain. On the floor beneath Edward was the tombstone of one Samuel Colman, who 'changed this life for eternity' at the age of eighty-four in 1653. I'd come across this phrase, or something like it, once before, on a hilltop churchyard in Cornwall; the sentiment had stayed with me for years. Samuel Colman must have known of the doings of Dowsing and his deputies, so must have seen how nothing is eternal, how even the most venerated of objects can be destroyed; yet the wall paintings above the altar here survived, first behind a coat of whitewash, then behind the panelling of a Victorian altarpiece, staying hidden until 1961. Brent Eleigh is so far out in the green, all it had to do was lower its head and Dowsing passed it by.

There were once wall paintings such as these all over Suffolk's churches, and many another county as well. You can imagine gangs of journeyman painters moving from one parish to the next with their treasured pouches of pigment; their oyster shells for mixing the paints; their brushes and a book of sample designs for their patrons to choose from. Brent Eleigh's patron is still there, kneeling down to the right of the altar, hands clasped in prayer, a giant Christ towering above him – or at least his ghost is still there, faded yet unmistakable. To the left, against what must once have been the blue of a star-spangled heaven before the pigment darkened, two angels waft incense toward a strange blank shape, which with the eye of faith you can see as once containing some particular treasure of the church; perhaps, with that asymmetric outline to it, a statue of the Virgin, holding the Christ Child on her hip – this is St Mary's after all. And there, over the altar, a much smaller human Christ hangs from his cross, eyes closed, with the Virgin to left and St John the Evangelist to right, both a-sway at what has come to pass.

Because this was how you did it, if you wanted to reach those whose comprehension of narrative was in images, not words, this was what you needed to give them: scenes from a story. Moments from a mystery play. And if your parish and its economy was as small as Brent Eleigh is still, you could hardly do so with a great multi-scene reredos, all oak and gold leaf and just waiting for the iconoclast's axe; instead you did so by having a Crucifixion painted on the wall – the simplest, most basic statement of the Christian faith there is. And because of that, it has survived when all those grander, more elaborate, have not.

But words still have their power. M. R. James is known today for his reinvention of the classic ghost story, many of the most profoundly chilling set in Suffolk, but in his lifetime he was a noted medievalist, and he was here, in Brent Eleigh, in the summer of 1891, waiting patiently (as I set the scene, in my imagination) for the keys to be found to a cupboard containing 'a curious library', bequeathed to the church very possibly by Edward Colman. The keys were located, the cupboard opened, and there within it was a twelfth-century book, still in its original wooden boards, of the life of St William of Norwich, written by Thomas of Monmouth, a monk of Norwich Priory. James, we are told, exchanged the book for 'money and fair words,' and off it went to a new home in the Bodleian Library – but what a perfect start to one of his own tales this would have been. James conjured up such sophisticated dread in his stories. In an essay in 1931 he set out what he thought were the principles of a good ghost story. First, do not 'use all the colours in the box'. The scariest thing in an M. R. James tale is what is only hinted at. It gives the reader's imagination space to work, to fill. Then, 'the more readily appreciable the setting is to the ordinary reader the better'. A small, quiet, empty church, then – would that do? 'The other essential is that our ghost should make himself felt by gradual stirrings diffusing an atmosphere of uneasiness before the final flash or stab of horror,' and in his tales they certainly do. Finally, James warns the would-be writer 'it will tax your best endeavours to forge the links between past and present in a satisfying way,' which is why James so often bridges them with a thing – a manuscript, perhaps; a mezzotint; an old whistle, oddly inscribed; an ancient book – and any reader of his stories will know that you remove such a thing, you take it from its resting-place very cautiously indeed, and only after having looked carefully behind you. It is perhaps as well, sometimes, to leave the mouldering leather bag, the blackened coil of twisted wire, where you found it.

*

We left Brent Eleigh by Cundys Lane, and found ourselves in a hollow way, where the path had sunk between its banks. I suppose the vagaries of geology would make it impossible to calculate the age of such paths by the depth of the sinkage (a hollow-way version of 'Hooper's Rule' for hedges, perhaps, where one woody species equals a hundred years of hedge, give or take) but if only one could. A flutter of movement at the tops of the scrubby trees, and what sounded like a very small bird shouting into a tin-can. A bullfinch, said Merlin confidently. We had to watch our feet. The farmer here had ploughed as close to the edge of the field as he or she could; added to which a mantrap of a crack, plenty wide enough to catch a booted foot, had opened up between the clay of the field and that of its verge. The path had almost disappeared. Dammit, honour the paths! Honour the feet that walked them!

One of our patron saints must have been listening. A turn to our route and no more field, no more corn-stubble and ploughed clay: instead, an avenue of trees – tall, straight, with fissured bark, one after another, as far ahead as we could see. What were they, poplars? Who planted them, the columns of this green cathedral, and why? We walked along it, voices lowered, marvelling. We reach out, when we find ourselves surrounded by this much of the natural world at once; we look for human meaning within it. We credit it with virtues and significance and power. We start to use the language of religious faith. 'It was high summer,' wrote Adrian Bell in *The Cherry Tree* in 1932, closing his rural trilogy:

> Tall as a single cliff stood the green-burdened elms, jagged and cragged with black sun-shadows, before which the gliding dove was like an allegory of faith in perilous places ... It was like some close rich tapestry before our windows in the early mornings, the thick-woven fantasy of slender leaves, edged with those that floated like weak hands and bless the air ...

When I got sick, what made me better was a hefty drug regime and a very clever surgeon, but walking served to remind me that outside the narrow focus of my illness there remained a world far bigger than me, with much beauty in it, and more, that this world would remain whether I was a part of it or not. And there was something comforting and salutary in being reminded of one's own insignificance. In *A Flat Place,* looking out over the emptiness of Orford Ness, Noreen Masud, herself a battler against chronic illness, records feeling how little the landscape needed her: 'It was indifferent,' she writes. 'I could have been a tuft of thistledown, blown harmlessly over the flat expanse, leaving no trace.' Exactly so.

You may disagree.

We came out of the green cathedral and at once were in a meadow full of flowers. God bless the farmer who let this lot run riot, even if they did plough out our path. There was hawkweed, there was cranesbill, there were dandelions (of course), there were daisies and scabious and cornflowers and thistles, and some other yellow thing, straggly but vigorous, which I am telling myself was the descendant of all that medieval woad, because it would be so pleasing if it was. And bees, making a noise like little tractors – bees everywhere.

There on the horizon was Lavenham's church of St Peter and St Paul. We had one more field to cross, where this time the path showed up as a worn line, like a pull of tailor's chalk, across a field of sugar beet, then here we were again among hedges of leylandii, not hawthorn, hedges that had been clipped and trimmed and shaped, and gardens that, as one of the Akenfielders rather meanly described them, 'look like shopping'. And to welcome us back into town, a pavement that did what so many Suffolk pavements love to do, which is swap from one side of the road to the other on a corner *that is completely blind*.

Lavenham's church sits on its hill like a monarch on a throne. It is surrounded by grass as smooth and bright a green as baize, and many roundly topiarised bushes that sit on the green like giant billiard balls. The best parts of the interior are its bones – the reeded columns of the nave, the march of the arches, all again the work, it is thought, of John Wastell, as at Bury. Then there is its clerestory, which is a miracle in itself – a layer of glass above the stone that makes the church seem even larger and more spacious within than it looks to be from without, as if that big Suffolk sky had come inside. It holds a mighty sense of calm, does Lavenham church, balm to the tormented spirit, I am sure. I'd live here, if I were a divinity. There is a poem about Lavenham church, written by one Rebecca Ribbans in 1822 and published after her death at the age of twenty-seven by her husband. It starts so unpromisingly:

Hail! Lav'nam Church! to thee my theme I raise –
Stupendous edifice of ancient days ...
... Thy striking form each passing stranger eyes,
Thy top, which seems to meet the low'ring skies,
O'erlooks fine sloping scenes and Kentwell Hall,
Long Melford Park, and Hedingham's Castle Wall.

But it is in fact rather extraordinary. It's a guidebook in verse, as Rebecca circles the church like a drone, itemising each noteworthy detail of its architecture from porch to 'matchless bell'; then each memorial within; then to specific graves within the churchyard, including that of her own sister. I wandered about the church running the poem in my head, ticking off this, ticking off that; I peered into the parclose surrounding the tomb of Thomas the Rich, which kept him as separate from his neighbours in death as his riches had cut him off from them in life, I cast my gaze down to the floor, but there were no flagstones, no well-worn granite slabs, no poetry. Instead there was sharp-cut Victorian terracotta, machined flat, set without flaw. I might choose Lavenham church were I divine, but if I wanted the right place to sit awhile with the human mystery of it all, it would be the tiny church at Brent Eleigh. We had walked there, and we had found good.

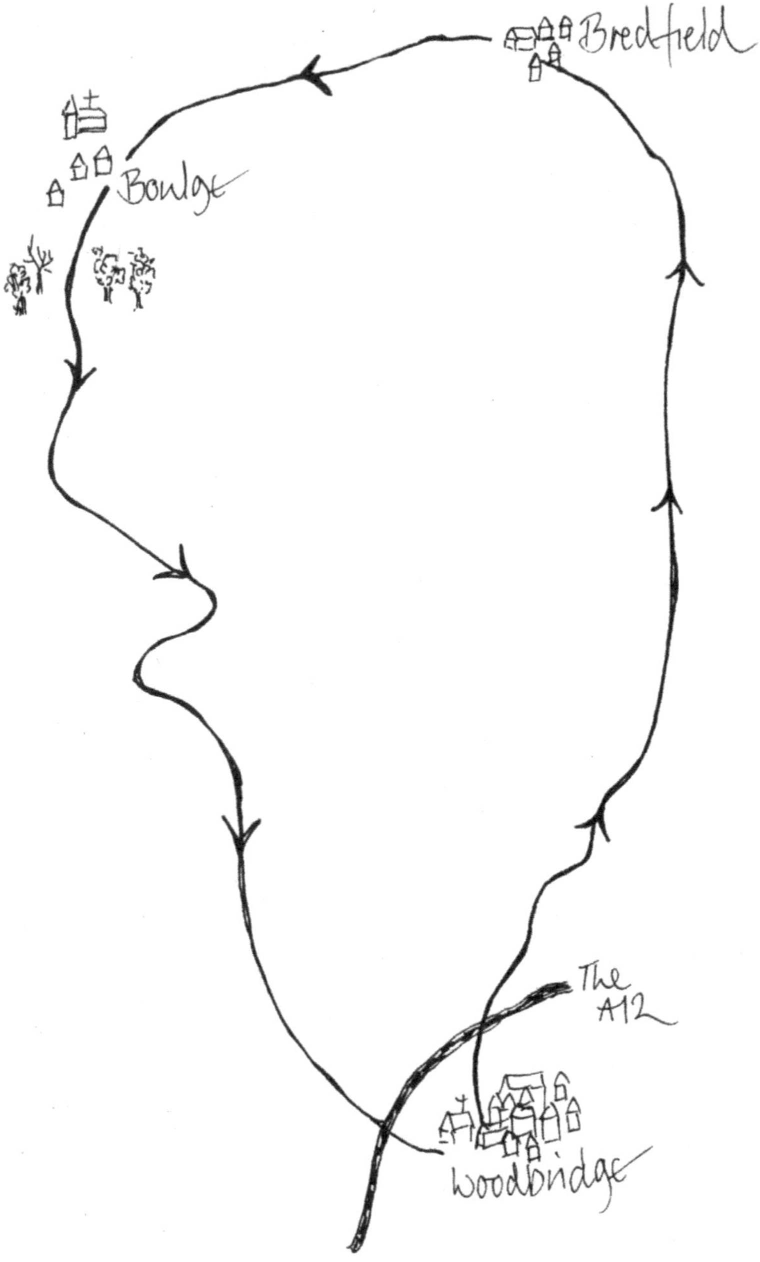
Bredfield
Boulge
The A12
Woodbridge

3

Edward FitzGerald and Me

Woodbridge

My father was born before the First World War. He had a whole other life before wife and children came along, and by the time we did, his ways were set. For example: he wore a shirt and tie and jacket every day of his life, because that was what men did. On the beach, or mowing the lawn, the tie might be shed, but that was as far as he would go. I don't think he ever owned, or wore, a T-shirt in his life. He was an indefatigable walker (one of the many reasons why it is such a regret he never met the Yankee), but at a speed – his speed – that meant wife and children would be left far, far behind. I don't think he was trying consciously to get away from us; that was simply his walking speed. When my mother upbraided him, as she often did, his reaction was miserable incomprehension – that he had angered her, that he was in some way at fault – but the speed didn't change. When he did argue back, which was rarely, his tactic was to argue the point next door to the one you were trying to have him understand, which was infuriating – passive, but complete, non-accommodation. He would, I think, have been genuinely baffled and offended by that description.

He had a strong baritone. He made up scatological ditties about the family cats and would boom out the opening lines to his favourite songs at a volume that was startling. One of his favourites apparently began with the word 'Hiroshima', which was shocking to me in the way that so much of the adult world is, when you're too small to understand it. Years were to pass before I discovered this was a folk-song classic, whose first line actually begins 'Here a sheer hulk lies poor Tom Bowling ...'

He was prone to declaiming favourite lines of poetry, too: 'And lo! The Hunter of the East has caught/The Sultan's Turret in a Noose of Light'. The words spun round me. What Hunter? What Sultan? What Noose of Light? Yet somehow, I knew what they meant: into my head there came an image of a city *somewhere* with towers and turrets and one higher than any other, and the dawn coming up behind it. I saw a finger of sunlight stroking up the tower. The words were like a spell. They were magical. I felt swoony. *The Rubaiyat of Omar Khayyam*, my father informed me (more magical words, wholly without meaning, but the sound of them full of enchantment), translated a hundred years ago by Edward FitzGerald, who had lived – this was the most fantastical thing of all – a cycle-ride away from us in Woodbridge, where my mother had her antique shop. *A loaf of bread, a flask of wine, and thou* – this was where that came from? Just up the road?

Totemic item by totemic item, Edward FitzGerald entered our house. First of all, there was an edition of *The Rubaiyat of Omar Khayyam* with illustrations by Edmund Dulac – visionary illustrations, full of detail and verve. All her life, even when its paper cover had dried out and cracked away, even when the pages were freckled with age-spots, my mother remained convinced this was a treasure of incalculable worth. (In fact, by 1909, when Hodder published this edition, FitzGerald's translation of the *Rubaiyat* had been a bestseller for decades. Copies are far from scarce.) Then there were a couple of little pencil sketches by Thomas Churchyard – the head of a horse, and a sow with piglets. 'He was FitzGerald's friend, you know,' my mother said, tapping a pair of picture hooks into the wall. 'When he died, FitzGerald gave his daughters a *fortune*.' Most significant of all, one day she came home from the antique shop with a strange, pale brown cane, peculiarly notched and noduled along its length. Made from a stem of Brussels sprouts, she told us, and yes, you could see where the sprouts had been detached, the scar each one had left along the stem. About six inches down from the top was a silver-plated fixing, where the cane unscrewed. In the longer bottom section, a thin, thin phial of thin, thin glass. In the top section, a tiny, narrow drinking glass. This, my mother swore, was Edward FitzGerald's very own walking stick, designed so that its owner might enjoy a warming nip of brandy whilst out walking.

There was no provenance, other than my mother's say-so, no 'E. F.' initials engraved on its knop, but it's not impossible that what she claimed was true. Relics of Edward FitzGerald were in local circulation for sure; in *The Time by the Sea* Ronald Blythe describes an encounter in the mid-1950s with the daughter of FitzGerald's housekeeper, Mrs Howe, who showed him the poet's shawl and inkpot. Then again, my mother had a habit of claiming things were true when in fact she only wanted them to be so. Or thought that they ought to be so. You can call this magical thinking; you could call her a fabulist. But FitzGerald's walking stick is how this object entered our house, and that is how it remained, through all its many showings and unscrewings, to reveal to the curious the long, long phial, and the dinky little glass. She never considered selling it. She was a bowerbird, my mother, and bowerbirds have trinkets they will part with and others they will not.

Of course, no-one can be absolutely sure that Omar Khayyam, eleventh-century Persian astrologer, wrote the verses that would become the *Rubaiyat*, either, but of such credos, history is made.

*

Say the words 'writer' plus 'Suffolk' to me, and the sum of those two is always FitzGerald: more than it is any other

Suffolk writer, such as Sebald or Crabbe or Blythe, or either of the Jameses, M. R. or P. D. Obviously, I have asked myself why, because we writers are always poking about in our own innards (our patron saint really ought to be St Erasmus – martyred by having his bowels wound out on a windlass). There was the connection with the walking stick, of course, but there was more. My father introduced FitzGerald to me, just as he introduced me to Dickens and Walter Scott and Thackeray and Tennyson and Robert Louis Stevenson and all those other writers of the Anglosphere that he had loved and grown up with himself. FitzGerald, like them, was the handing on of a gift. 'The Moving Finger writes,' my father would begin, in a baritone growl, raising his own finger in warning:

... and, having writ,
Moves on: nor all thy Piety nor Wit
Shall lure it back to cancel half a Line,
Nor all thy Tears wash out a Word of it.

I was an anxious kid, and anxious kids are problem solvers. If the terrifying Finger had to move on, the solution was obviously to have it write something less tear inducing next. When Cheryl Strayed hit a crisis on her epic ramble, her option – her only one – was to keep walking. For me, the solution was to keep writing. The solution was always that.

Or, it was to escape into a book. The book I wandered

about in time and again, as *Thoughtlands* came into clearer and clearer focus, was FitzGerald's letters. FitzGerald is a prince among letter writers. There is the same almost unwitting candour, the same revealing of the self as there is in Pepys's *Diary*, and as with Pepys, no matter what your opinion of the man's actions, how can you not come to care for someone who shares themselves with you so completely? 'My dear Barton,' FitzGerald wrote in May 1845 to Bernard Barton, Woodbridge's Quaker poet and father of FitzGerald's wife Lucy, 'I was at a party of modern wits last night that made me creep into myself'. I know that feeling; who does not? 'My dear Allen,' he confides to a schoolfriend (the letters are like conversations), 'once every week, at least, I feel spurred on by a sort of gathering up of feelings to vent myself in a letter upon you'. He is blunt to a fault: 'I saw you yesterday when you called, but I was not fit for company, and felt I could not be bothered,' was a note sent to a local bookseller. He shares the woes of age: 'NB I am going bald'. 'I have got the fidgets in my right arm and hand (how the inconvenience redoubles as one mentions it)' and he relishes everything each new season has to offer:

> ... the East winds may again plunge us back into winter: but the sunshine of this morning fills one's pores with jollity, as if one had taken laughing gas ...
>
> Yesterday I walked (not a common thing for me) eleven miles; partly over a heath, covered with furze bushes just

> come out into bloom, whose odour the fresh wind blew into my face ...
>
> The reign of primroses and cowslips is over, and the oak now begins to take up the empire of the year and wear a budding garland about his brows. Over all this settles down the white cloud in the West, and the Morning and Evening draw toward Summer ...

And he mocks himself, and what he calls his 'Robinson Crusoe' life:

> I read of mornings; the same old books over and over again, having no command of new ones: walk with my great black dog of an afternoon, and at evening sit with open windows, up to which China roses climb, with my pipe, while the blackbirds and thrushes begin to rustle bedwards in the garden ...

We do live like Robinson Crusoe, we writers, every chance we get, happily solitary on our island of one.

Yet at the same time, nothing mattered to FitzGerald more than his friends. Overlapping circles of male friendship surrounded him all his life, with him as their fixed point. One of the first such companions, when the poet was still a child, was Edward Moor, he of *Suffolk Words and Phrases*, who started in FitzGerald a love of Suffolk dialect of his own.

Years later, FitzGerald would create his own list of *Sea Words and Phrases,* including such beauties as 'dead as a mitten', 'clock-calm', and 'Betty', for one over-nice in putting things in order: 'He go betty, betty, bettyin' about the boat like an old woman.' At boarding school in Bury St Edmunds (a welcome relief from what sounds to have been a horrid childhood) his friends would all go on to become wordsmiths of one sort or another – the journalist William Bodham Donne, the editor James Spedding. At Cambridge his companions included William Makepeace Thackeray and Alfred Tennyson. Once back in Woodbridge (which he returned to seemingly without any thought of making some kind of a way in the wider world), another circle was created that included Bernard Barton; George Crabbe II and III (son and grandson of the poet); Francis Hindes Groome's archdeacon father Robert; and Edward Byles Cowell, another Suffolk boy and – having sparked up FitzGerald's interest in the Persian language in the 1850s – godfather to the *Rubaiyat*. Even in death (he died in 1883) FitzGerald brought people together: the first edition of his *Letters* came out in 1894; Francis Hindes Groome's *Two Suffolk Friends* came out in 1895; John Glyde – a local historian of considerable note, in his day – published his *Life* in 1900, with a foreword by Edward Clodd; and Clodd himself was one of the founders of the London Omar Khayyam (or OK) Club in 1890, of which Sir Arthur Conan Doyle was a member. (*The Moving Finger* – could there be a more perfect title for a Sherlock Holmes mystery than that? Instead Agatha Christie used it for a Miss Marple mystery in 1942.) Ripples from the *Rubaiyat* reached admirers as far off as Ezra Pound; no doubt they are travelling still.

The more I read of FitzGerald, the more I felt my way into him, the more I felt I had met someone very much like him before. The incomprehension as to what others might expect or need from him; the inability (or refusal) to accommodate. 'Something a little strange,' is the phrase that crops up in John Glyde's *Life* of 1900, 'a studied defiance of some of the little conventionalities which are supposed to make the wheels of society run smooth.' The blinkered trudge forward, when better choices lay to either side. The turning in on oneself. The impatience this might give rise to in those around you. The novelist Edmund Gosse described FitzGerald as 'a man of taste in easy circumstances, and until he was forty years of age he was nothing else whatever.' As with my father, FitzGerald would, I think, genuinely have been baffled by that description, and offended.

My father died in 2003. My mother has had twenty years without him; most, I hope, happy enough, but the last years, not. Dementia unmoored her – like a balloon dropping its sandbags, one by one, she floated further and further away from reality and from us. Then came a stroke, a tiny one, but one like the single stone that slips out from under your shoe and ends by sending you purling down a mountain-side. There was a stay in one hospital, then another; then a nursing home where they tried to feed her lying down, so she developed aspirated pneumonia. Back into hospital again. Then another nursing home. Every time I see her, there is less and less of her, both physically and in her apprehension of the world. Where she is now, she is as happy and is cared for as protectively as an infant in its cot, but she's a changeling – a fragile little being who lies curled in her bed like a child in the womb, or as if already prepared for burial under some Suffolk tumulus. And such care, as anyone who has been through this or is going through it knows, costs all you have. Everything had to be sold – her cottage, and everything in it, all the antiques she and my father had collected and in which they had taken such pride. The Thomas Churchyard sketches, the Dulac *Rubaiyat*, and what may or may not have been Edward FitzGerald's walking stick; all gone.

Let us walk.

*

'Woodbridge,' writes Defoe, 'a little town beautify'd with neat buildings' – and so it is, but for me it is also one I go back to lugging much baggage. My plan for this walk was to make it a kind of homage to FitzGerald, to follow the route set out by William Dutt in his *Literary Associations*, and go from Woodbridge to Bredfield, where FitzGerald was born in 1809, over to Boulge, where he is buried, and then back into Woodbridge again. But if you begin a walk with baggage, the walk can go one of two ways: either the baggage falls from your back like Christian's bundle in *The Pilgrim's Progress*, and like him you do three leaps of joy; or, as Stevenson puts it, you find yourself walking 'with the hag'. Twin and I drove into town, we parked the car, we walked up the Thoroughfare; I stood in the doorway of what had been my mother's antique shop, with the lion that had of course been there for centuries above my head, and I mourned – for her, in the death-in-life, the limbo, of dementia and for me. And for my Twin as well, as the day we made this walk was the anniversary of her own mother's death. We were a doleful duo, as we made our way up the Thoroughfare, overfull of thought. Hans, of course, was oblivious, trotting along beside us, fleecy fur a-ripple like the fringe on an old-fashioned lampshade.

We could have performed a small diversion and gone straight on at the crossroads at the top of the Thoroughfare and down Cumberland Street, in which case, had we persisted to No. 23, we would have been outside Barton's Cottage, his 'nutshell house', as he termed it; in passing No. 6 we would have passed where Churchyard lived with his seven daughters and two sons during a rare period of financial solvency. Churchyard trained as a lawyer, although he was convinced his true vocation was as an artist; he managed to go bankrupt in both professions, but for a brief moment his house in Cumberland Street housed paintings by John Crome, George Morland, Constable, and Gainsborough. And yes, FitzGerald did assist his friend's daughters after his death. My mother had that absolutely right. But instead, we turned uphill, past St Mary's church ('went to church there this morning, where everyone sat with a purple nose, and heard a dismal well-meant sermon; and the organ blew us out', FitzGerald wrote to Tennyson's brother Frederic in 1844). Here was the Market Square, where my mother's life as an antique dealer began with a stall in the Thursday market, in the shadow of the pint-size, Flemish-looking Town Hall; and where, at 10 Market Hill, FitzGerald lived from 1860 to 1873 in what Dutt describes as 'a little room over a gunsmith's shop', quietly relishing what the poet himself called 'all the faded tapestry of a country town life: London jokes worn threadbare; third-rate accomplishments infinitely prized; scandal removed from dukes and duchesses to the parson, the banker, the commissioner of excise, and the attorney.' What did he care. He was famous by then – the *Rubaiyat* had come out in 1859, and having sold hardly a single copy in its first year, was then discovered by the painter Dante Gabriel Rossetti, then the poet Algernon Charles Swinburne, then the Victorian polymath John Ruskin. FitzGerald's fame and his friendship would be enough to bring both Tennyson and Thomas Carlyle to this small market town. Tennyson stayed at The Bull, which closes off Market Square at one end as The King's Head does the other, while Ruskin was enthused enough to write fan-mail:

> I do not know in the least who you are, but I do with all my soul pray you to find and translate some more of

> Omar Khayyám for us: I never did – till this day – read anything so glorious, to my mind as this poem ... and that, & this, is all I can say about it – More – more – please more – & that I am ever gratefully & respectfully yours.

Swinburne, thrown into even greater literary frenzies, is meant to have written 'Laus Veneris' in the *Rubaiyat's* honour. It begins:

> Asleep or waking is it? for her neck,
> Kissed over close, wears yet a purple speck
> Wherein the pained blood falters and goes out;
> Soft, and stung softly – fairer for a fleck ...

How FitzGerald would have smiled at that. Or squirmed. FitzGerald's sex life is something of a mystery, but not that much.

> ... men of keen sensibilities and thoughtful character generally limit their friendships to a small circle, and give to the members who compose it a friendship of the most exclusive, intimate, and unreserved kind. This was the case with Fitz-Gerald [sic]. His friendship was more like love. The persons to whom he was drawn, by a kind of magnetic attraction, were his companions in school and college days; and the confiding intimacies begun thus

> early caused each object of his regard to be pressed close to his heart, and embraced with a brother's love.

If you say so, Mr Glyde. During the years spent on Market Hill, FitzGerald's heart was all given to a Lowestoft fisherman, Joseph Fletcher, twenty years his junior and described by his admirer as 'the finest Saxon type: with that complexion which Montaigne calls "vif, Mâle, et flamboyant"; blue eyes; and strictly auburn hair, that any woman might sigh to possess.' 'Some good rough soul who works my boat' was FitzGerald's public description of Fletcher, known as 'Posh', and their relationship was an exercise in tolerance all round – on FitzGerald's part that Posh was married, with two children, and a liking for the pub; on Posh's part that this older man, this local oddity, haunted the beaches and quays in order to keep tabs on him; and above all on the part of that circle of FitzGerald's friends who surely must have had a name, or names, for this. 'A favourite sailor' is the gloss given by Francis Hindes Groome. William Dutt declared sniffily that 'The friendship between the two very different men must necessarily have been one-sided, and the space devoted to it by several writers who have dealt with FitzGerald's life in Lowestoft is largely wasted,' and with that, dusted off his hands. Dutt might have been taking aim here at James Blyth's *Edward FitzGerald and Posh* which went out into the world the year after Dutt's own book. Blyth's account of the friendship, whatever it was, between FitzGerald and

'Posh' is a considerable oddity in itself, as was its writer: born in 1864, Blyth was an early creator of science fiction, and was troubled to the point of obsession by the notion of war between England and Germany. His *The Swoop of the Vulture* of 1909 would be spoofed by P. G. Wodehouse, also in 1909, as *The Swoop! or How Clarence Saved England*. Blyth's 200-page account exists, so he said, to prove FitzGerald was not a 'sulky misanthrope' but a man who could show 'consistent tenderness and delicacy of spirit to his fisherman partner'. The book was 'honest criticism by man of man.' It demonstrates on every page how difficult it was to write the story of a love affair when every stricture of society forbade you from saying one man – elderly, socially the superior – was in love with another, who for his part seems to have dealt with his admirer mostly with an amused acceptance of the manifold differences between them.

Yes, I know, that was a long *divert*, even for me, but studied defiance of society's expectations was indeed a part of the man, and should be acknowledged. You get the feeling that among FitzGerald's friends it was understood that such habits as draping himself in an old blanket when he went out were not to be criticised or commented upon, nor was his diet (bread, fruit, tea, good ale) to have attention drawn to it. In nineteenth-century Suffolk it was of course far easier to get away with such behaviour if one was moneyed and well born. FitzGerald named the boat in which he and Posh sailed so contentedly round the coast and up and down the Deben as the *Scandal*, because, he said, nothing in Woodbridge travelled faster. Posh himself, seventy years old and a widower when Blyth came calling, died in 1915 in the workhouse at Oulton near Lowestoft. This grates, somewhat.

Dutt also says it is not more than half an hour's walk from Woodbridge to Bredfield House, where FitzGerald was born. *He lies.* Twin and I walked from the Market Square, still in the Tudor core of Woodbridge, down Angel Lane to Bredfield Street, which sounded almost too good to be true – and was. Surrounded by nineteenth-century red brick, we walked on. North Hill led us up, where Angel Hill had led us down. Bredfield Street became Bredfield Road, still with no sign of Bredfield itself, and now we were surrounded by the vanilla of a modern housing estate. These tree rings of development surround every town – you walk from new into old, going in, and the reverse going out. 'The petty race of Squires who have succeeded only use the Earth for an *Investment*,' FitzGerald spat in 1861, 'cut down every old Tree: level every Violet Bank: and make the old Country of my Youth hideous to me in my Decline.' Stevenson's hag was gripping my elbow tighter with every step by this point. Yet another horribly busy road (worse was to come), and we found ourselves in Foxburrow Nature Reserve, surrounded by cherries and blackberries, elderberries and hops, and with this sense of that busy and almost invisible life going on all around us. There was a lizard, for a microsecond, on our path; there were rustlings to left and to right; there was a butterfly, a

Gatekeeper I think, doing its tipsy wander, looping about our heads. A rabbit showed us its heels; by the side of the path, moon white, a parasol mushroom had reached its full flat stretch. There was a stile to make our way over (a guarantee you are in proper countryside), and then another, and then another pair of walkers, an elderly couple, laughing, bidding us good day, and as Stevenson puts it, the weathercock went about and the hag was gone. Foxburrow or 'boro Hall was a Red Cross hospital during the First World War; I hope it did those damaged, bandaged souls wandering its grounds with the shells from the Somme still going off in their heads as much good as it did me.

We were not, however, free of the modern world quite yet. There at the end of our path was the A12, which runs round Woodbridge like a moat and which would have to be crossed if we were to get any further. And contrary to all my phone had been telling me, there was no crossing, no drawbridge here.

Christian had his Black River, we had this. We picked up Hans and ran, made it to the other side and there waiting for us was a no doubt one-time inhabitant of the nature reserve, a deer – not a whippet-sized Muntjac but a red deer, full grown, a doe – hurled into the side of the road and completely smashed, the poor thing. The cars roared past behind us. Who drives at that speed? Who needs to? I hope the impact smashed the car that hit it, too. Muttering dark thoughts and imprecations against the driver, we took the field path before us, toward Ufford and Bredfield, past pines of such spindly, spidery, twiggy growth they would have made a fitting lair for the becloaked apparition from M. R. James's story 'The Tractate Middoth', with his bald head 'and the streaks of hair across it [that] were much less like hair than cobwebs'. Perhaps in James's imagination, that's what these trees were. In the story, Bredfield becomes Bretfield, and the hero, William Garrett, taking a short cut across the fields, witnesses the apparition, 'a mass of blackness', exact its terrible revenge upon the villain, Squire Eldred. After the inquest into the squire's mysterious death, Garrett makes his way back across those same fields and sees, just where Eldred had fallen, 'something dark ... Looking closer, he saw that it was a thick black mass of cobwebs; and, as he stirred it gingerly with his stick, several large spiders ran out of it into the grass.'

On a first visit to Dunwich, on the coast, I had attempted to share with Twin the plot of M. R. James's 'Oh, Whistle, and I'll Come to You, My Lad', this being one of the most spine-chilling tales ever committed to paper, in my view. It had been a late afternoon, late in the year, and the cliffs at Dunwich were darkening, and the light over its marshes was getting thinner and yellower by the minute. I was rather relishing my scene-setting for her, in the way one does when sharing something scaresome, with no thought to the possibility that Twin's imagination might be just as suggestible as mine, until she begged me not to tell her more. I decided not to share my 'Tractate Middoth' thought with her, as she strode happily ahead with Hans at her heels.

*

One of FitzGerald's few original poems was composed in honour of Bredfield White House, where he was born. It begins,

Lo, an English mansion founded
In the elder James's reign.
Quaint and stately, and surrounded
With a pastoral domain.

So far, so tum-ti-tum. FitzGerald was pragmatic about his abilities as a writer, compared to those of so many of his friends. 'I have not the strong inward call, nor cruel-sweet pangs of parturition,' he wrote, although clearly he knew that 'strong inward call', that bug in one's head – he has to have done.

There were eight little FitzGeralds, all told, and the entire family, so said Edward, were mad, but he at least knew that he was. They were of such wealth it seems to have quite unhinged them. His father was an amiable duffer, a country squire content to jog-trot through life, but his mother (from whom her children used to hide) had the money, and the pretensions, of being a society hostess. An 'elegantly ostentatious woman of the scentless-rose sort' was how a friend of her daughter described her. This might be one of the most spiteful judgements I have ever heard one woman make of another.

It is extraordinary how unlucky the FitzGerald family houses have been; one might almost imagine some kind of M. R. James-type curse over them. A stray V1 rocket, of all things, demolished FitzGerald's birthplace; the cottage he occupied in the grounds of Boulge Hall burned down in 1923; Boulge Hall itself, which the family moved to from Bredfield, was demolished in 1955. (Little Grange, to which he moved in his old age, still stands, however, on Pytches Road in Woodbridge, complete with blue plaque on its Suffolk-pink wall.) So our goal here, no more than a convenient turning point, was Bredfield's church of St Andrews, where we were greeted by a notice asking us in the friendliest, least alarmist manner possible to 'keep clear of the large churchyard trees', as one had dropped a whopper of a branch.

From the outside, Bredfield Church reminded me very strongly of the church I grew up with. The same flint, the same stone mouldings framing the glass of the east window, the same stepped tower (although ours was Tudor brick). The resemblance was even stronger inside – the same cool air, cool to the point of feeling damp; the same slightly bitter aroma in the air; the same kneelers hung on the back of the pews; the same mysterious notices of church business long past; the same oak panel up on the wall giving the wording of the Lord's Prayer, should one forget. In our village church we had the Creed and the Ten Commandments too. 'Hear what comfortable words our Saviour Christ sayeth unto all who truly turn to him,' our elderly vicar would intone, repeating what would have been heard within the church since 1662, and we were comfortable, and comforted too, every Sunday, like the pressing of a reset button. Then came his successor, and the liturgy for Series III, and the word of God was replaced by the wording of a committee. I hated it. My mother hated it. Half the congregation hated it. It was tone-deaf, it was ugly, it was trying to be everything to everyone, and it ended up being nothing to anyone. The congregation diminished noticeably. From my eleven-year-old standpoint I disliked the new vicar, too. There was a noisiness to him, and a hail-fellow well-met heartiness that suggested disregard, a barging through, and raised in me the suspicion that his being crossed would not be a pretty thing to see. Also, if man could come along and change the word of God as he pleased, what was His/Her/Their/Its word in the first place?

How much easier a business faith would have been in the days when George Crabbe II was rector of Bredfield, and FitzGerald would walk over the fields from Boulge to sit and smoke and debate with him. The debates must have been lively. For the son of a poet, Crabbe had no liking for poetry, while FitzGerald was a sceptic where religion was concerned. 'I wish that the not being happy without the prospect of Heaven were a proof of Religion,' he wrote to John Allen, a friend from Cambridge, 'but alas! 'tis no more so, than a beggar's not being happy without a penny in his pocket is a proof that there soon will be a penny in his pocket: it will make him happy to believe so, but the penny is as far off as ever.' Perhaps the *Rubaiyat* drew FitzGerald into the translating of it in that its tone so chimed with his own wry, pessimistic attitude toward the hereafter: 'that inverted Bowl we call The Sky', the poem exhorts us through FitzGerald,

> Lift not thy hands to IT for help – for It
> Rolls impotently on as Thou or I.

Yet the *Rubaiyat* still enchants and consoles. What can one do, under so huge a bowl as a Suffolk sky, but continue, insignificant, un-responsible and thus bundle free, upon one's way?

Exit through the corner of the churchyard, and there before us, down through the centre of a meadow with trees massed to its right and more on the horizon, was the wide, green path – wide enough for a tractor, the tough grasses beaten flat – across the fields to Boulge.

*

You can make a case for FitzGerald not having translated the *Rubaiyat* at all. 'He never pretended to literal translation, nor would he have been interested in it,' says his more recent biographer Robert Bernard Martin. 'It was fidelity to the spirit of Omar he sought, not to the text.' In FitzGerald's words, 'To keep Life in the Work (as Drama must) the Translator (however inferior to his Original) must re-cast that original into his own Likeness, more or less: the less like his original, so much the worse: but still, the live Dog better than the dead Lion.' 'In his own likeness' for FitzGerald meant taking the quatrains that most appealed to him from the original, re-ordering them and turning them into something else. '... at all costs,' he would write, 'a thing must live: with a transfusion for one's own life if one can't retain the Original's better.' He did the same with the books in his library, literally cutting out the sections he felt they could do without and re-ordering what was left; and with Bernard Barton's poems, for the posthumous edition of which he was editor. You could almost argue that FitzGerald's *Rubaiyat* is fan fiction; a bringing together of admirer and source. That is all part of its allure: 'Try to find out why the FitzGerald *Rubaiyat* has gone into so many editions,' Ezra Pound exhorted himself as a sort of poetic quest. To discover why, come with me: in 1913 Pound, the arch-modernist-to-be, had a job working through the notes of the philosopher Ernest Fenollosa. These included Fenollosa's rough translations of Chinese poetry. Pound spoke hardly a word of Chinese, but using Fenollosa's writings as a starting point he was inspired to create *Cathay*, one of the peaks of twentieth-century literature: a collection of fifteen Chinese poems not so much translated as transmuted into English. Poem speaking to poet, in other words, just as with the *Rubaiyat*. In the introduction, Pound/Fenollosa writes that 'Poetry ... must appeal to emotions with the charm of direct impression, flashing through regions where the intellect can only grope.' These are big, many-layered, gnarly ideas, which Pound sought to unpack in leisurely footnotes, including a description of the instinctive understanding of Chinese pictograms that he witnessed in two of his artist friends – one of whom was Henri Gaudier-Brzeska, the other of which was ... Edmund Dulac. I was wildly expounding all this to Twin, carried away by my own excitement – from my mother's bookshelf to Ezra Pound! – when the path we were following simply disappeared. Instead of that line of tailor's chalk across the field, acres of sugar beet.

I'd had something like this happen before, when walking in the Rocky Mountains. The trail I had been following then was so faint that at my feet it was invisible, but looking ahead one could just make it out, a line running along the crest of the ridge, as if what I was following was not the path itself, but the mark where it had been erased. Would this be the same? I peered ahead. Nothing. Was I fooling myself, that I knew this landscape, could work out a way across it, to where I wanted to go? (Said FitzGerald, in a letter of 1841: 'I walk about in the fields where the people are at work, and the more dirt accumulates on my shoes, the more I think I know.') I checked my phone again – no, there the path was, in a satellite photo across a field freshly harvested, and there it bloody well was not, in front of us, not erased but ploughed up, seeded, and now grown over. I get it, you don't want to have to divide your field in two, but how hard is it, to leave that slightly wider gap between two rows as you plough and seed, to put the path back where it is meant to be? Said Twin, imperiously, gesturing at the thick green leaves, 'We will walk over it,' but I am a tractor girl, I was brought up to respect the farmer's crops, so no, we walked round the field and found the road, and continued to Boulge that way. It was only maybe an extra quarter mile, but we resented every single step of it, in particular that member of our party with legs six inches long.

Boulge Church, of St Michael and All Angels, is off the road, up one track, then right and up another. You will know you are there when, most unexpectedly, you see a giant redwood in front of you, and beyond that a small iron gate with curlicued finials and a rather startling cross, painted white, on its top rail, like something you might place on the coffin of a baby. It is very tree-girt, Boulge Church, and the churchyard was wonderfully unmown when we were there in August, with an ancient mowing machine from who knows how long ago that had been left leaning up against one of the gravestones and was now quite buried in the grasses – a Suffolk vanitas, if you like. As the *Rubaiyat* says,

> Into this Universe, and why not knowing,
> Nor whence, like Water willy-nilly flowing:

And out of it, as Wind along the Waste,
I know not whither, willy-nilly blowing.

There they are, the FitzGeralds, in a tripartite memorial inside the church – to left the father, John; centre-stage and with the largest memorial in the place, the formidable mother; to her right the daughter, who died at eighteen. The church is dominated by them. But Edward FitzGerald is not with them. Nor is he in the flinty Gothic family mausoleum that rears itself out of the churchyard, in which Ronald Blythe records being allowed to view the FitzGerald family's brass-studded purple coffins, ranged along shelves inside as in some everlasting larder. FitzGerald's grave is beside the mausoleum, in pinkish marble, and it bears the inscription 'IT IS HE THAT HATH MADE US, AND NOT WE OURSELVES'. The poet gets the last word.

In front of his grave there is a rose bush encircled by chicken wire. It announces itself as having been raised in Kew Gardens from the seed of the rose that blows across the grave of Omar Khayyam himself, and of having been planted in 1893, but I think not. It may possibly be a grandchild of one of the six Blythe saw being planted one November day in 1972 by the Persian ambassador no less, on the orders of Persia's last shah. It did not look happy. Some of its leaves were yellowing, as if trying to mimic the sunlight of which it must surely be deprived, where it is under the churchyard trees, and the sandy heaths of Suffolk are a long, cold way from the gardens of Nishapur. It looked stunted; it certainly is not one such as FitzGerald described:

> Look to the Rose that blows about us—'Lo,
> Laughing,' she says, 'into the World I blow:
> At once the silken Tassel of my Purse
> Tear, and its Treasure on the Garden throw.'

This one did not blow. It sulked. It looked as if it wanted to be anywhere but here.

Our route back would be via Hasketon. The path beyond the church was admirably clear (hats off to whoever sees to it), over more green sward and punctuated by splendid trees – oaks full of leaf, and others, older, doing that thing oaks do where they self-amputate a limb, so that one stark, dead branch protrudes from the whole like the bowsprit on a sinking ship. There were others (elms, I suspect) that were entirely gone, mere skeletons. One oak was managing to do both – one half round with leaf, the rest of it leafless, with whitened branches dropping their scrolls of bark and broken to half the length they would have had in life. Does a tree know it is dying, or like the Lavenham willow, that it has taken a mortal blow? If it does, would it care? 'The known interprets the obscure,' says Fenollosa, through Pound; 'Nature furnishes her own clues.' 'These were his trees,' said Twin reverently, which I think is almost the same thing. According to Martin's biography, FitzGerald's way of working was to 'read over the relevant sections several times until their broad outlines were fixed in his mind, then to go for a long walk and work out the stanzas.' More writers, more walking. Hammond Innes would go to what he called the Great Wood:

> ... so many scenes worked out, a whole story line refashioned, a piece of dialogue framed on the mind's tongue, so clear I might have spoken it aloud – the trees, the dog, the grasses and the birds, all unseen, my mind locked in on the problem of the day. A mile walked and nothing seen but what is in the mind. What a waste of a beautiful day, yet what satisfaction if just one line has fallen into place or a character found himself again, the story moving on.

Wordsworth did the same. Solnit includes a splendid description of Wordsworth at work from an unimpressed local witness up in the Lake District: 'He would set his head a bit forrad, and put his hands behint his back. And then he would start a bumming, and it was bum, bum, bum, stop; then bum, bum bum, reet down till t'other end; and then he'd set down and git a bit o'paper and write a bit.' That would have been FitzGerald for you too, that old blanket knotted round his shoulders, humming and muttering and banging out the rhythm of his lines of verse on the ground with – yes, why not? – with his walking stick, while his great black dog nosed round the trees. We were walking, literally, in FitzGerald's footsteps, sharing his shadow, discussing his meter, his rhyme scheme, his steps, his words; his character, his reputation (worldwide, even now). Said Twin, 'Where is Hans?'

We were standing on our own. We looked for Hans. Our small white dog was waiting yards behind us. Seeing he finally had our attention, Hans lay down. In vain did we try to fool him with the 'One, Two, Three!' game ('Come on Hans – one, two, *THREE*!'). In vain did we attempt to restore him with a biscuit and a drink of water, then to lure him on. He lay with paws either side of his muzzle, and gazed at us in deep, deep, sorrow at our foolishness in thinking we could get him moving again by any ruse short of putting him on a sled. But, we were ready for him. You could hardly get away with this with a wolfhound, but for a dog of Hans's size, there is such a thing as a doggy rucksack. The offer of a biscuit had him stand on it; we zipped it up around him before he could escape, hoisted him on to Twin's shoulders, and there he was, a Sealyham papoose.

It was a very pleasant thing, to give entertainment to so many as we walked back into Woodbridge. A couple bicycled past us with cries of 'Aaaaw!' trailing over their shoulders. Those in cars pointed, smiled, and waved as they went past. But it was a long mile or so back, and I was doing it without the weight of a dog on my shoulders. We found ourselves walking beside the wall of Woodbridge School, which FitzGerald also attended, but rather than debate the poet's childhood, all we wanted to talk about was what we were going to have for supper. Hazlitt had that exactly right. And what we were going to drink, once we got home. A gin and tonic. A glass of wine. A gin and tonic *and* a glass of wine. The size of the bar and of the buffet, shimmering, mirage-like, ahead of us, increased with very step. We stopped at a corner shop to grab a couple of bottles of water and give Twin's shoulders a rest, and her phone rang. 'Lieber Bruder!' I heard her exclaim, sounding pleased. Of course, the anniversary of her mother's death. I moved a little away, to give her privacy. I felt that fog of mournfulness rising round me once again.

I was in London when my father died. When I saw him, his body was already in a coffin at the undertakers, dressed in this ridiculous pale blue nightie, like a choirboy's hassock, with a frill at the neck. I sat with him, I put my hand into his (it still felt like his hand); I wept a lot; I talked with him of I do not know what. I sat there for so long the undertaker came to check on me. When at last I said goodbye, I kissed his forehead, and it was like kissing a marble wall, so solid and so cold. And he was one side of it, and I was the other.

When you are young, death happens to other people. At some point in life that changes. One of the unexpected if unasked-for boons of illness is that you wake one morning in the small hours understanding it will happen to you too.

Twin was done with her phone call. I think she saw the sorrowful slant to my face. She clipped Hans onto his lead.

'We shall go home and make supper,' she announced, and I felt a little of the sadness leave me, eased away by thoughts of cooking with a friend, and eating with them, and a glass of wine on the sofa with a small, tired dog beside you who, even if he isn't yours, has come to trust you enough to go to sleep with his head on your knee. 'This was a good walk. We have earned it.'

This is irrevocable, was what that solidness, that marble coldness said. *It doesn't care how much you mourn, it isn't going to change. Deal.*

I am doing the best I can. This is part of it.

And so was that.

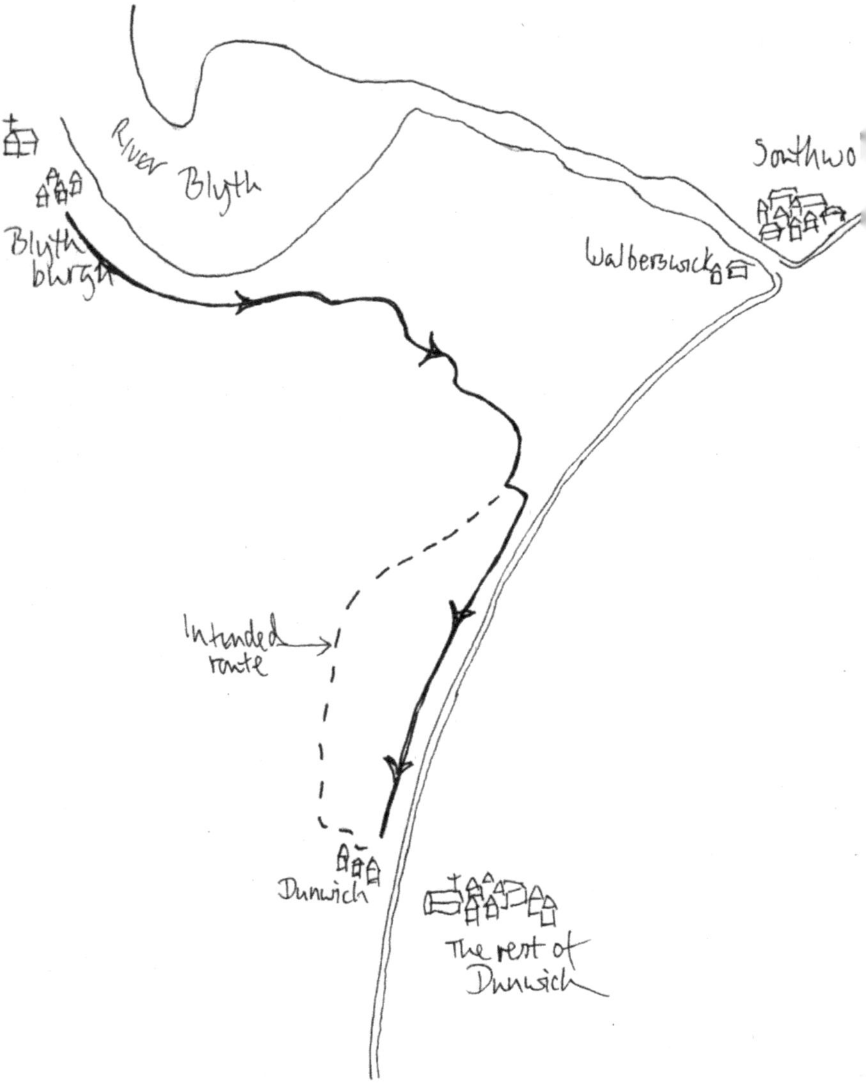
River Blyth
Southwo
Blythburgh
Walberswick
Intended route
Dunwich
The rest of Dunwich

4

Heart Songs

Dunwich

I HAVE LOST TRACK of the number of times the North Sea has tried to drown me. The shelf of shingle off the beach at Felixstowe that dissolved beneath my feet like a bath cube; the sea that received me, sour as embalming fluid, and into which I sank from sheer surprise. I must have started fighting back at some point (perhaps when it filled my ears?), and I probably did not go straight down into it as unprotestingly as I do now in memory, like the corpse of some eighteenth-century sailor, sewn into a sail for a winding sheet and weighted with chain, but that is how I remember it – the bubbles from my nose streaking past my eyes, and when I turned my eyes up, the see-through ceiling of the sea itself between me and the sky. Or in Norfolk, at Blakeney, the running tide that ran so much faster than I could swim, racing out from the River Glaven and carrying me with it. I remember the faces of the adults on the quayside, looking down, watching me battling toward them, each one thinking *should someone do something here? Should I be that someone?* as the tide swept me out toward the sea. It was a moment that solidified a strong childhood belief: other people can never be entirely trusted, and adults least of all.

Or perhaps I have imagined it. Memory is a living thing; it shifts and changes. It is water held in your cupped hands, and try as you might, it will leak away. Imagination, meanwhile, is a hydra. It may not be the thing that makes a writer, but it is the thing, I think, that determines what kind of a writer you will be, and mine is such that seeing *Jaws* kept me out of the River Deben for a year, unshakable in my secret conviction that the only Great White ever to find its way into the North Sea would swim up the Deben and find me. In compensation, I could have written a stomach-clenching description of its attack – the tug backwards, the dark cloud of my blood enveloping me, and the head and above all the rotating eye of the creature as it came through the dark cloud at me. I imagined my arms disappearing into its mouth. I pondered with sickly irresistibility how one died in a shark attack – shock, or loss of blood, or were you in fact, piece by piece, literally eaten alive. My imagination gave all this to me, as if I'd find good use for it, rather than it coming to completely rule me. To this day, I am a very, very nervous swimmer. I need a toe on the bottom. Even as an adult, swimming in a friend's pool, at the back of my mind there lurked the dark possibility that at the back of their shrubbery, there was an undetected alligator (this being the U.S.), that would silently gain the water and choose me upon which to launch its attack. I honestly don't know if this is neurosis or ego.

It is no different on dry land. We had a stuttering bus service to our village, which one autumn evening deposited me at the crossroads with a walk down an empty road to get home in that winter dark that swells up from the edges of your vision – Magritte darkness, you might call it, perhaps. It was a walk of maybe 500 feet, say 150 metres or so. Within a few paces of setting off, my brain popped up for me, like a piece of toast, this, from *The Rime of the Ancient Mariner*:

> Like one, that on a lonesome road
> Doth walk in fear and dread,
> And having once turned round walks on,
> And turns no more his head;
> Because he knows, a frightful fiend
> Doth close behind him tread.

I cannot remember, at the age I was then, even having read *The Ancient Mariner*, but there it was, and I can still summon up the hopelessness of my terror – and my sense of the utter unfairness of having to keep walking forward to get away from it.

There are any number of shivery weirdnesses in Suffolk, many (but not all) having to do with the sea. There was the half-man, half-fish creature caught off Orford Ness, that place that is it itself half-land, half-water. At Dunwich, the goal of this walk, there are clifftop ruins and streets of drowned houses over which you may swim, if you are a far better swimmer than I, as birds once flew over their roofs. There were the children who appeared seemingly from underneath the earth in Woolpit, back toward Bury, in the twelfth century, with their subterranean, green-tinged skin; while our churches must make space for wodwos, wild men from deep in the green, carved on their fonts, and peculiar hooded figures or 'poppy-heads', as they are known, that live on the ends of the pews. There is Black Shuck, the demon dog as big as a calf, who haunts the Suffolk lanes and may be the incarnation of the Devil, but who has always sounded to me as he were the embodiment of misery instead – the ultimate 'black dog'. No wonder this land created M. R. James, with his tales of the inexplicable, thus doubly chilling, that all begin in such innocence and end in such horror. You can no doubt foresee the delight with which my rogue imagination threw itself upon such descriptions as this: 'with the odious writhings of a wasp creeping out of a rotten apple there clambered forth an appearance of a form'. This is from James's 'Mr Humphreys and His Inheritance'. It's the 'wasp' moment that lodged with me, and is lodged with me still, but James is merely turning his engines over here. You wait till we get to those clifftop ruins.

Then there is all that Suffolk can do by itself. There are those thick hedges hiding unexpected openings of all sorts.

There is pale sacking left on the far side of a field (but is it?); or a golden sandbag on Aldeburgh beach that on closer inspection becomes a small dead seal, its flippers pressed together like supplicating hands, the skin already gone from its head, the startling pink of the exposed flesh and the gulls circling above. There are those deserted churches that now do stand alone. There are uneasy lopsided gravestones; ancient gargoyles, from the mouths of which project demonic heads, like the xenomorph in *Alien*. There are the tricks, in this flat land, that distance can play on you, those castling moves within the landscape, which is how Suffolk is used not in the book but in the movie of Ian McEwan's *The Child in Time*: a figure appears in front of you, but how did it get there? There are shreds of mist hiding in the hollows of the roads, one of which (at least, we told ourselves it was mist) shot straight up into the sky in the headlights of the car as a schoolfriend's mum drove us back over the emptiness of Brightwell Swale one night and disappeared as if it had never been. There are reedbeds, head height, within which waters gurgle and unseen creatures splash. There is the sea itself, especially at night, when its noise is all you hear and when it seems to have taken over the world: 'three nights ago I looked out at about ten o'clock at night, before going to bed,' FitzGerald wrote to Frederic Tennyson in the winter of 1844,

> I heard a continuous moaning sound, which I knew to be, not that of an infant exposed, or female ravished, but

> of the sea, more than ten miles off! ... people here think that this sound so heard is not from the waves that break, but a kind of prophetic voice from the body of the sea itself announcing great gales. Sure enough we have got them, however heralded. Now I say that all this shows that we in this Suffolk are not so completely given over to prose and turnips as some would have us.

If you wish to scare yourself silly, Suffolk is an excellent place to do it. Just as well, therefore, that the Yankee came along with me for this one. Let us walk.

*

I rediscovered walking with the Yankee. I walked as a child, on family holidays, but then I had no choice; I walked in my teenage years, when living out in the Suffolk countryside there was no other option if you wanted to get anywhere – that, or a bicycle, or cadging a lift – but I had never come across anyone who walked so regularly for the pleasure of it before him. Every other soul I know sits down with a drink to relax: the Yankee goes for a walk. Ronald Blythe talks of how, as a writer, listening was a large part of his craft, and since I have known the Yankee, walking has become a part of mine. Blythe talks too of how he found he heard more when not actively listening; I find I see more when not looking, when the rhythm of walking first unfocuses then frees my gaze, and my thoughts start to appear in single images and then as words, and then that inner narrative is off and building, step by step, phrase by phrase.

It peeved me greatly, therefore, that this walk had to start by us both getting into a car and driving off to Blythburgh, but from Aldeburgh, the distance to Blythburgh would in itself have taken us a day, and the plan for this walk was to head along the River Blyth until we reached the sea, turn south, and end up at Dunwich. Not only had I miscalculated how far away Blythburgh is, nor had I made allowance for the endless switchbacks and the roads reduced to single file and the mess being made of this part of Suffolk by the building of the Sizewell C nuclear power station. It was a shock. The closeness of the roadworks to Leiston Abbey, for example (as we in our taxi inched forward, car by car) – the green skin ripped away, the orange earth exposed, and the Abbey, which used to stand a little downhill at the end of its own track, now with cars within yards of it. So much for the child, Theresa, coming here as she does in P. D. James's *Devices and Desires* to commune with and remember her dead mother:

> They ... would cycle here together and walk in companionable silence among the ruined arches or stand hand in hand where the altar must once have stood, hearing what those long-dead monks had once heard, but more remotely: the melancholy booming of the sea.

All you would hear standing there now is the grind of cars changing gear. Yes I know, we must have electricity, we must have power; no longer being able to experience the setting as P. D. James did does not count for much (especially as in the book she relocates the whole of this part of the Suffolk coast to Norfolk), but it counts for something, and the thousands of trees that have been felled count for even more, and the promises from the powers that be that everything will be restored to how it was are so idiotically stupid as to count for nothing – how can you restore trees that were decades, if not centuries, old when they were felled? How to restore the generations of creatures that would have lived in them? 'Did they at least allow the archaeologists to have a look around?' I asked our taxi driver as we went past more skinned earth, more red and white tape curving in the breeze, and he said yes, they did, and very glad he was of it, the archaeologists being the only ones who drank, who needed lifts to and from the local pubs. Those building Sizewell C, he said, put not a penny into the local economy: not in the shops, the pubs, or the restaurants. They sat in their block-booked holiday cottages all week then disappeared at the weekends, and their malign influence was even buggering up smartphones and Wi-Fi in this part of Suffolk. It did not bode well for our walk.

Every time I go to Blythburgh Church it is being readied for a wedding: long boxes of blooms piled around the font, the wedding organiser in a frock, everyone else rushing about in jeans; the church full of scents from the flower-filled buckets off to the side and the sound of the snip of secateurs. It must be a lovely place in which to say your vows. Ronald Blythe was deeply attached to Blythburgh Church (of course he was – look at what they share in the way of a name), and was here in what sounds like that heightened state of intense internal composition when the real world and the one in your head wash over each other like tides, but instead of preparations for a wedding he found a young man of his own age, mid-thirties, in his coffin, on trestles in the chancel. 'A woman arrived and swept and dusted round him,' Blythe reports. It would not have been the first time she had done the same, I am sure. Those gangs of church cleaners, the women of the parish – the flower ladies, the dusters of hymn books, the polishers of brass lecterns and of altar crosses – they must have seen everything.

Blythburgh is another church with a clerestory; all that expensive glass drenching the interior with light, which tells you quite how tony the parish was once upon a time. There was a priory here too, there were Augustinian canons, there was money. All that went with the Reformation. Now there is this light-swept building, with the I-washed-up-here air to it of all the flint churches on this pebbly coast; and its ceiling, where angels – what that bastard Dowsing left us of them – smile down on you and flutter their wooden pinions, the word of God in faded red and green behind

them; and its floor of Suffolk pamments, which I urge you to lie down upon, press one cheek to, and look across, is a wonder. Each tile – terracotta, pale pink, chalky gold – is like a square piece in a patchwork quilt, with the floor rising and falling in gentle undulations as if the sleepers beneath had turned in their sleep, then settled back again. I shared this notion with the Yankee, and it was rewarded with a warm smile of enjoyment, so I share it here with you, now. There are ways in which the workings of his head and mine interlock as perfectly as one of those Japanese woodworking puzzle-joints; there are ways in which we could not be more different. My universe is pantheistic, not to say anthropomorphic; his is agnostic, rational. He is steady balance, he is a clock; I am a needle with a long, long thread. On my tombstone I would like to exchange time for eternity; on his, he has suggested 'These worms tickle.' If we end up side by side, what a pair we will be. But then our whole relationship is the reverse of the norm. He lives in Brooklyn, I am based in London, so for us, unlike most other couples, it is time together that is the novelty, not time apart. Other people, when they are together, go out for a treat; our treat is to pull up the drawbridge and stay in. Thank God he is a writer too; he can spot when I, like Blythe, have disconnected from the world and in that heightened state am writing in my head, and it freaks him out not at all. We are like two cops dating each other: we are the only people who would understand where the other one is coming from.

The glue, the bridge between us, has always been words. When we are apart (say, three-fifths of the year), we write to each other twice a day, morning and evening. Maybe 500 words apiece, of everything we might otherwise share face to face – big, small, life-changing, life-affirming, quotidian, downright daft or wholly incomprehensible to any other soul. We use all that twenty-first-century tech can provide us with to do something as old-fashioned as Abelard and Eloise. We have been doing this for fifteen years. Two thousand words a day, back and forth, 220 days a year – by now it's something between 7 and 8 million of them. Ten times the Bible. Seven times all the Harry Potters. Twice as many as Agatha Christie, in all her incarnations. You see the math of it set down like that, it's a wonder we have ever found time to write anything else.

Back to Blythburgh. Forty years after the Reformation, one Sunday in 1577, came Black Shuck, in an enormous storm of summer lightning that 'cleft the door', brought the timbers of the steeple crashing down on top of the font, and killed a man and a boy among the congregation cowering in the pews. He manifested at Bungay Church as well, on the same day and perhaps at the same instant (accounts differ); it seems mighty restrained of him, after all that, to have done no more than leave two dark claw-marks on the north door, marks so very much like those that might have been caused by a pair of incautiously positioned candles. There was also a port at Blythburgh, before the river sidled away. Now, it has the wretched A12 – not a moat, as it is in Woodbridge, but a bisection, as you cannot get from one side of the village (the church) to the other (the river) without having to cross it. If you are following us on foot, gentle reader, *prenez garde*. We took our chance, and then we were safe on the other side of the road with the traffic thundering away behind us and me turning my phone, like a water diviner's hazel-rod, to line up the map on its screen with the landscape before us (the Yankee is chilled with my complete lack of a sense of direction too). Two women had crossed in front of us, then they disappeared apparently into the hedge. 'There!' said I, and we followed them onto a track between the fields and down to the river, the edges of our path washed with mauve and aromatic with Russian sage and startling with bright red montbretia, an escapee from some Blythburgh garden. A Gatekeeper butterfly fluttered past, wings sadly ragged; a chainsaw screamed into life behind us; as we neared the marsh its noise was replaced by the *bump, bump, bump* of heavy bass from Latitude Festival, taking place over the river – the reason, no doubt, for the solid traffic on our journey up here. 'So much,' said the Yankee drily, 'for the peace and quiet of the countryside.' On my phone, my route-map was telling me with increasing desperation to pause navigation, to re-centre, to make a U-turn, but no. I wanted to get down to the edge of the marsh, and to the edge of the marsh I would go. The path itself made no such fuss – on it went, bracken to one side as high as our heads and to the other, reeds and little stunted oaks, and beyond them the river and the islands of the marsh, which always look to me as if you could sit on them as on a magic carpet as they floated you away. One bore a heron, like a birthday candle.

The poet Swinburne – he who was thrown into such raptures by the *Rubaiyat* – was here in the 1870s, on these very marshes, rhapsodising over the 'cloud-clogged sunlight, cloud by sunlight thinned.' So was Henry James of all people, in 1879, extolling the landscape of the Sandlings, as this part of Suffolk is known; 'the way the brown hamlet really disposes itself, and the grey square tower of the church, in just the right relation, peeps out of trees.' What brought them here was the railway, which was bringing more and more visitors by the 1870s, first to holiday here, in Aldeburgh, in Walberswick, in Southwold, even in ruined Dunwich – England's Atlantis – then to go home and read about it. If this landscape is what your soul demands, it will let you know. People are pulled here. 'I wandered about seeing the land joining the sky in the huge way it does in Suffolk. I thought of Constable,' says the schoolmaster in *Akenfield*:

> I did national service but I still thought of the Suffolk land and sky ... I used to say to myself, I'll go there. I meant, I'll stay there. This sounds sentimental, doesn't it? I went to an art school but nothing I learned hit me as this landscape does. The truth of the matter is that I don't see the village, I see the sky touching the land and nothing ever interrupting.

The thump of Latitude Festival was muffled now. All there was, was green: brambles so thickly interwoven they might have surrounded Sleeping Beauty's castle; and bracken interlaced above our heads and growing so vigorously you might fancy you could hear it doing so as you passed. What we heard instead, unmistakably, was a buzzard, that faraway, strangled-sounding 'garrrrr!'. 'That's a buzzard?' queried the Yankee, peering up, and thinking no doubt of the cowboy version (bald headed, two-metre wingspan) circling over the bluffs of Arizona. He shaded his eyes, but the buzzard by now was far beyond the reach of human sight, although no doubt it could still have made out the pair of us perfectly well. 'That's a really wimpy little voice for such a big bird of prey,' said the Yankee, who is a city boy, with urban expectations that size and sound should correlate. Another and much noisier disturbance and a golden retriever came bounding toward us with a blissful smile upon its doggy face, a dog muddy to the chops, a dog muddy to the Plimsoll line, and its rather less happy looking but almost as muddy owner. 'Did he have fun?' I asked, meaning the dog, and the owner replied, heavily, '*He* did ...' What a difference four legs makes.

There are always side roads, walking in the city. You turn down an alley and a completely different set of options opens up to left and right, but in the country, there is just the one path, like this, and if you stray off it, you are like a medieval serf straying into places where you don't belong, one of which here would be the river. 'Watch your step,' the Yankee cautioned, black water glinting below us to either side. Is there any culture where water doesn't connect us with an underworld? Celtic warriors broke spears and shields and buried them in pools and rivers, the Styx waits for us all, and sometime around 1937, while her sister was teaching in Ipswich, Stevie Smith, she of 'Not Waving But Drowning', thus a woman who had thought much, I suggest, about the ambivalence of water, wrote a poem in which she rowed with Death down not the Blyth, but the River Deben. It is perhaps the only poem in which my birthplace is ever likely to feature, and it ends:

> Oh happy Deben oh happy nights and night's
> companion Death
> What exultation what ecstasy is in thy breath?
> It is as salt as the salt silt that lies beneath.
>
> Flow tidal river flow, draw wind from the east,
> Smile pleasant Death, smile Death in Darkness blest,
> But tarry day upon the crack of dawn; thou comest
> unwished.

She added a drawing, as scrappy as one of Edward Lear's, of the two of them, she and Death, together in a rowboat, as if as proof of it having happened. Death looks like one of the cowled pew-ends from Blythburgh Church.

Turn right off the footpath along the Blyth, and *The* Street (another one) will take you into Walberswick, famously one of the prettiest and most expensive places to live in the entire country. 'A haunt of artists,' says M. R. James in his *Suffolk and Norfolk*, unwittingly coining a new collective noun. It has an inn right on the beach, so close to the sea that at night it creaks in the wind like a ship, where the Yankee and I stayed on one of his earliest trips to England, when we were obeying the rule that says you must give your beloved a crash-course in all the years of your life before you met. He had taken me round Massachusetts, and I introduced him to Suffolk and got him addicted to fish and chips.

This is a book about strokes of the writer's pen rather than of the artist's brush, but there must be exceptions. One such is Philip Wilson Steer, who in Walberswick in 1887 painted *The Bridge*, a work of almost Munch-ian unhappiness. A man and a woman stand on a bridge over a river. She looks out to the sunset; he gazes at her. Something dire has gone wrong between them. It was a starting point for Maggie Hemingway's 1986 novel *The Bridge,* with its agonising dissection of a love affair that cannot be between Steer and the fictitious Isobel Hetherington. Hemingway was born in Orford; her sense of the Suffolk coast and its air, its skies, its trees, its dunes, its spirit goes through *The Bridge* like sunlight, but she also got right inside Steer's head, and what happens when you untie yourself from the rest of the world and are living up there, creating. This is Emma, Isobel's lonely youngest daughter, watching the artist sketch:

> She thought how strange the expression on Philip's face had gone, it had become laced up with a taut urgency, and his eyes had got smaller and fiercer so that they

seemed to look right inside her without noticing her face at all.

I do begin to understand why so many people, when I'm writing in my head, ask me if I'm quite all right. Inspiration looks so much like a TIA.

We could have walked to Walberswick, we could indeed, but in my view a true country walk should include as little tarmac as possible, so we crossed The Street by what at first looked like nothing more than one of those indents in the verge where the council keep sand for the icy roads of winter, but which turned out to give onto more sandy Suffolk heath with the line of a footpath in the grass. Another couple came toward us, younger than we, he a little ahead, she fluffily pretty and a pace behind, as if she was letting him forge the way. They looked the tiniest bit put out to encounter us, although we exchanged the obligatory greetings, the nod of the head. Once they were out of earshot, the Yankee whispered, 'I can feel that look on my face too.'

'What look?'

'The one that says, "what are you doing here on our path?"'

True – this is *our* walk, we say. We have no wish to share it with either tarmac or other walkers. It is ours.

We were coming up to Lodge Road (a second option into Walberswick, should you wish) when we found ourselves again sharing the path, but this time with the first of what turned out to be four pairs of dragonflies, all duelling it out in mid-air. Were they fighting or mating? They were very large, that was for sure, the sound of their wings like someone humming through paper and comb. 'They're like biplanes,' marvelled the Yankee, 'like mini World War I biplanes!' and I rewarded him with a warm smile of appreciation of his own. The dragonflies, flashing sometimes green, sometimes brown, sometimes yellow in a sunbeam, took no notice of us at all – perhaps in their hyper-world of aerial acrobatics we were invisible. A field of sable sheep, all head down amongst their grazing, also took no notice of us, then just to prove this was heathland indeed, mound after mound of purple heather. Heather is such a boring plant in the garden, a real sign of *I've given up* on the part of the gardener, I always think, but these were growing in mounds as big as beanbags, and in a suitably psychedelic '60s purple. A little further on there was a sign announcing 'Corporation Marshes' – how unromantic for the landscape we were about to enter.

*

A confession.

Technically, the route for this walk was to carry us along the edge of the farmlands, the Sandlings, with the Dunwich marshes (the Dingle Marshes, to be strictly correct) to our left. If you follow this route online, you will see exactly where we should have turned right, and the dividing line between green of trees and edge of fields, and the wine-coloured marsh; the borderline, Swinburne called it, comparing the terrain beyond to Hades. But we walked in amongst the reeds and seemed unable to walk ourselves out.

We did not, to be honest, try too hard – at least, one of us did not. I knew we only had to keep following our noses and we would reach the sea, and I love reedbeds. I love the way they make you feel both exposed and enclosed all at once, the way people on the path ahead appear and disappear as the path winds and curves behind the reeds all out of sight; where within them you experience what Sebald called 'the immense power of emptiness'. I like the slight air of the uncanny they engender, the possibility of small happenings beyond explanation; they give me that same pleasing mix of sensations as watching something scary on the telly with the arms of the one you love wrapped round you: indulging yourself in being scared, instead of actually being it. We could watch the wind come at us, over and through the tops of the reeds, sometimes bringing us the sounds of Latitude again, and sometimes, growing slowly louder, we caught the sound of the sea pulling through the pebbles of Dunwich beach. There was a ruined windmill, which delighted the Yankee, movie-obsessive that he is, by looking so very like the one in Hitchcock's *Foreign Correspondent* (it truly does), and yet another path back through the reeds to Walberswick, out of which an extremely buff, pinkly wind-stung, shirtless young soul came running as we passed, thudding past us and away. If you were to go down that path through the reeds back to

Walberswick and the River Blyth, you could cross the Blyth to Southwold itself, either by ferry or further upstream at its Bailey bridge.

Something about Walberswick, for all its prettiness, its current celeb status, seems to generate a deal of adult angst. Renamed 'Steerborough', it is the setting for Esther Freud's *The Sea House* – another love affair between an artist, Max Meyer, and Elsa Lehmann (neither of them native to this flat land), whose history is unravelled years afterwards by Lily, another newcomer. Southwold fares even worse. Sebald hymned its Sailor's Reading Room, but before him Orwell set *A Clergyman's Daughter* here as a revenge upon the town, Southwold being the place his parents chose to retire to. Dorothy, the daughter in question, has such a wretched relationship with everything around her – her father, the town, religion itself – that she is driven to stick pins in herself like a witch's poppet. Orwell is vicious in his depiction of

Southwold – the lecherous golf-playing middle-aged men and the kind of women who visited his sister's tea room in particular – despite the fact that the Adnam's brewery sits in the town, regularly scenting it with the smell of hops, a smell the writer loved: 'Like a wind blowing from oceans of cool beer,' he said. To add to the case against what writers will do to write, Brenda Salkeld, the local woman who was the model for Dorothy, dismissed Orwell's fact-finding for *Down and Out in Paris and London* as 'all that business about being a tramp was just ludicrous.'

Julie Myerson uses Southwold as the setting for *Something Might Happen* (it does – both adultery and murder) and *The Stopped Heart* (the past coming out of the past: I warned you, history like a mugger). Penelope Fitzgerald set *The Bookshop* in Southwold, influenced by the 'Solebay Bookshop' in which she worked after she and her children and war-damaged, indigent husband decamped to Suffolk. 'I still miss, and shall always miss, the wide shining horizons of East Suffolk, and the sight of the rooks and seabirds balancing themselves on endless currents of air,' she wrote in 1989, but the fictional bookshop she creates is cursed, first by a poltergeist and then by the casual cruelty of the fictional Southwold's 'ruling classes, facing one way, grazing together.' They destroy Dorothy, the bookshop's owner and, in the most genteel way possible, run her out of town. Worst of all, P. D. James, forgetting Adam Dalgliesh, used the beach at Southwold – *Southwold*, of all places, with all its pretty beach-huts – as the setting for a 'Quietus' ceremony in the dystopian *The Children of Men*, where the elderly are taken out and drowned. Heaven help you if you try to intervene, as does the book's protagonist, Theo Faron:

> He heard a voice, quiet, authoritative, almost gentle, 'Let it be, sir. Let it be.' ... a blow on the side of his head and [he] fell. He was aware of the harshness of pebbles grinding into his face, of the overwhelming smell of salt sea water, of a pounding in his ears. His hands scrabbled at the shingle, trying to get a hold. But sand and shingle were sucked away beneath him. And then another wave struck and he felt himself dragged back into deeper water. Only half-conscious, he tried to raise his head, tried to breathe, knowing that he was close to drowning. And then came the third wave which lifted him bodily and flung him among the stones of the beach.

It is the sea that is behind all this, both metaphysically and geographically. On this coast everything you have can be swept away without warning, and has been, over and over again. Defoe wrote of Dunwich, of how by 'a private pique of Nature (which has set no fixt bounds to the incursions of the Sea) the greatest part of it is swept away by the violence of the waves' (nonetheless, as a notorious 'rotten borough', for centuries it sent two MPs to Parliament), and of Southwold, 'At high water, it is so encompast with the Sea, that you'd take it for an Island, and wonder that 'tis not all overflow'd.' In 1953, of course, it was. Sebald imagined the awful confluence of storm and high tide that finally bore Dunwich off into the sea in 1328, but he could just as well have been describing that of 600 years later:

> ... as darkness fell those living around the harbour fled with whatever belongings they could carry to the other town. All night the waves clawed away one row of houses after another. When dawn came the throng of survivors stood on the edge of the abyss, leaning into the wind, gazing in horror through the clouds of salt spray into the depths where bales and barrels, shattered cranes, torn sales of windmills, chests and tables, crates, featherbeds, firewood, straw and drowned livestock were revolving in a whirlpool of whitish brown waters.

Three hundred and fifty-eight people died in the floods of 1953 (many, many more on the North Sea's Dutch coast). In *The Sea House*, the hut where the lovers meet is physically washed out to sea, and in the chaos afterward Esther Freud disposes of Ella's objectionable husband, while a smaller, later inundation washes Lily and her boyfriend Nick together again. P. D. James also used a memory of the 1953 floods as a *deus ex machina* to close *Unnatural Causes*. There is a high-water mark on many souls here, as there is on many of the buildings, and it never goes away. Said Henry James in his essay 'Old Suffolk':

> The coast, up and down, for miles, has been, for more centuries than I presume to count, gnawed away by the sea ... Few things are so melancholy – and so redeemed from mere ugliness by sadness – as this long, artificial straightness that the monster has impartially maintained ... It stretched, within historic times, out into towns and promontories for which there is now no more to show than the empty eye-holes of a skull; and half the effect of the whole thing, half the secret of the impression, and what I may really call, I think, the source of the distinction, is this very visibility of the mutilation ... There is a presence in what is missing – there is history in there being so little. It is so little, to-day, that every item of the handful counts.

I may have no sense of direction, but even I can't lose the sea. Here we were at the beach, with Dunwich before us, huddled away from the ruined abbey on its hill as if the hubris of the ruins might yet be dangerous. It was, however, quite a bit further off than I had expected. This might take a while.

Trudge, trudge, trudge.

Dunwich itself may be better known now, as the town that disappeared beneath the waves, that it was even in its medieval heyday. It's the potency of that image of all those drowned churches, tolling away beneath the waves. It has been celebrated by local poet after local poet, both in the *Suffolk Garland* of 1818 and in its successor, the *New Suffolk*

Garland of 1866, edited by the Ipswich historian John Glyde, in which the poetry is interspersed with chatty gossip and local lore. Glyde includes this, by James Bird, a one-time miller who lived 6 miles (10 kilometres) inland in Yoxford and was father of no less than sixteen:

> Where the lone cliff uprears its rugged head,
> Where frowns the ruin o'er the silent dead,
> Where sweeps the billow on the lonely shore,
> Where once the mighty lived, but live no more;
> Where proudly frowned the convent's massy wall,
> Where rose the gothic tower, the stately hall,
> Where bards proclaimed, and warriors shared the feast,
> Where ruled the baron, and where knelt the priest, –
> There stood the city in its pride – 'tis gone!

There is also another, contemporary, *New Suffolk Garland*, published in 2022. It does generate the words, this county.

Trudge, trudge, trudge. The charm of walking on shingle is soon exhausted, and so is the walker. The noise of your feet on the stones means conversation has to be conducted at a shout; as does the constant crash of the sea, and the shingle banks here aren't high enough to shelter one from the wind, either. Dunwich seemed to be coming no nearer; nor was that part of the beach where I could make out inroads of grass crossing the shingle, which would at least give a bit of variety to the trudging. To distract ourselves, we looked for hagstones.

Hagstones are flint, with a small irregularity in which an even smaller stone gets caught; and stars die, and empires rise and fall, and towns disappear under the sea, and eventually enough time passes for the one small stone to wear a hole right through the flint and out the other side. Hang them above your bed and they prevent nightmares. Hang them in a stable and they stop witches sneaking in and riding the horses at night. They are a powerful artefact, supposedly, against evil beings of all sorts. I am proud to say I found a pair of them, and, given that we were slowly getting nearer to Dunwich's clifftop graveyard, just as well.

Trudge, trudge, trudge ... When those churches went under the sea, they did not quite manage to take their graveyards with them. I remember as a child (or I think I do) walking along under the Dunwich cliffs and seeing coffin boards sticking out of the earth, and on top of the cliff itself there were gravestones embedded in the bramble. Swinburne spoke of seeing 'ruins and bones protruding seawards through the soil of the crumbling sandbanks'. In M. R. James's most terrifying tale, 'Oh, Whistle, and I'll Come to You, My Lad', a Professor Parkins is rash enough to remove a small metal whistle from the ruins atop such a cliff and is at once aware of something seemingly pursuing him along the beach. Back at his hotel, he is fool enough to try the whistle out. 'It had a quality of infinite distance in it, and, soft as it was, he somehow felt it must be audible for miles round.' He goes to bed, and is at once hag-ridden by nightmares of the most terrifying sort:

> A long stretch of shore – shingle edged by sand … in the distance, a bobbing black object appeared; a moment more, and it was a man running, jumping, clambering over the groynes, and every few seconds looking eagerly back. The nearer he came the more obvious it was that he was not only anxious, but even terribly frightened … now there began to be seen, far up the shore, a little flicker of something light-coloured moving to and fro with great swiftness and irregularity. Rapidly growing larger, it, too, declared itself as a figure in pale, fluttering draperies, ill-defined. There was something about its motion which made Parkins very unwilling to see it at close quarters. It would stop, raise arms, bow itself toward the sand, then run stooping across the beach to the water-edge and back again; and then, rising upright, once more continue its course forward at a speed that was startling and terrifying …

Long ago, I had described all this to the Yankee, just as I had done with Twin. 'Feh,' was the only reaction. I sat him down with the story and made him read it. All he did was shrug.

'But don't you see?' I said, 'It's Freddy Krueger, *avant la lettre*!'

Another shrug.

'But it's terrifying! Alone on a beach, completely exposed, with that thing hunting you—'

'Sweetheart,' said the Yankee, 'it's not.'

The man has no soul. Trust me, it is petrifying; read it yourself.

Trudge, trudge, trudge ... Strange plants now surrounded us as we slogged along, plants with thick, blue-grey leaves and branches of strange globular growths of some sort, raised aloft. Sea kale, so my phone told me. They looked like triffids; you could image them uprooting themselves from the shingle and walking inland. At last we were upon the narrow ribbons of grass stretching across the shingle. The café was near enough to discern cars in its car park. As we staggered over the last few hundred yards, breathing hard, ears singing from the wind, blood sugar about to crash, we passed behind a group of hardy souls picnicking up on the shingle bank, one of whom, good God, had been pushed there across the shingle in a wheelchair. We fell up the steps into the café forecourt. 'I'll have to call for a taxi,' I said, leaving the Yankee in the queue for food.

It was the weekend of Latitude Festival. Obtaining a taxi took time. When I came back, the Yankee had found us a table. 'The taxi firm say it'll be forty minutes at least,' I told him.

He was sitting there with knife in one hand, fork in the other, and on the plate before him a slab of battered cod the size of a wing from one of Blythburgh's angels. 'Not a problem,' he said.

Our journeys usually end in lovers' meeting. This one ended in fish and chips on the beach.

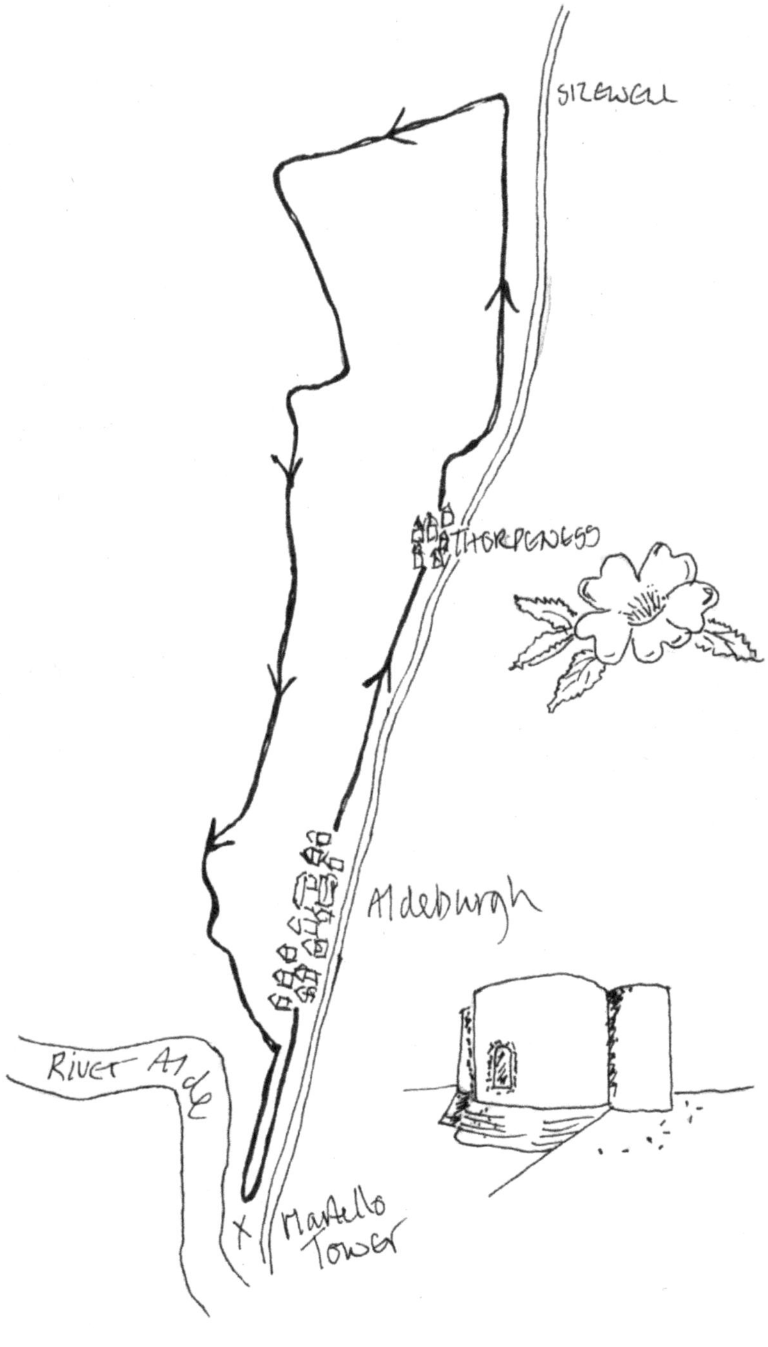

SIZEWELL
THORPENESS
Aldeburgh
River Alde
Martello Tower

5

Ferric Affinities

Aldeburgh

ARE THERE LEY LINES for writers, and if so, what do we call the places where they converge? Writer after writer has come to Aldeburgh, this place where land gives way to sea, and made a pause, sometimes for years. Their lives and words pile up on top of each other, until you can imagine an Aldeburgh built of lines of print rather than brick or stone. Wilkie Collins, writer of the bestseller *The Woman in White* and connective tissue for so much of Aldeburgh's literary history, was here in 1862, working on what would become *The Woman in White*'s follow-up, *No Name*, although annoyingly he credits Broadstairs in Kent as being the place where much of its writing was done. All the same, a significant portion of *No Name* is set here, in this 'quaint little watering place', as Wilkie describes it, with its 'fanciful little houses ... possessing here and there, as horticultural ornaments, staring figure-heads of ships doing duty for statues among the flowers.' And he got the mirage-like qualities of Aldeburgh's horizon perfectly – the way that it does indeed seem to be 'higher than the land', especially if you first encounter it as I did, small enough that you still have an adult holding your hand. 'A sea standing like a wall' is how Ronald Blythe described it a century later, with the boats on the horizon like lost toys left on top of the wall in case their owners should ever return. Even now, the first sight from Aldeburgh beach of that sequinned topline of the sea sparkling on the horizon or, if the weather is otherwise, dividing pale grey from dark, still makes some joyous thing rise within me. This is the horizon I grew up with. *Spiritus loci*, this is home.

So who were they, these writers? A mere skim across the top will net you Ruth Rendell and Patricia Highsmith; Ronald Blythe, who worked here on the first of its festivals; and the ubiquitous East Anglian spook-meister M. R. James, whose grandparents owned grand Wyndham House beside Aldeburgh's church of St Peter and St Paul and who (according to Blythe) is meant to have seen his first ghost within the church itself. God knows there are enough of the lost at sea named in the churchyard but not buried beneath it for some homesick shade to be wandering here. Kathleen Hale, who created Orlando the Marmalade Cat, knew Aldeburgh; she sent Orlando, his 'dear wife', and their family of kittens here to 'Owlbarrow' on holiday. A generation or so below them is the Darwinist and folklorist Edward Clodd (1840–1930), who came to Aldeburgh as an infant with his sailor father, and who had six small brothers and sisters buried in the churchyard. Not only an Aldeburghian himself (he authored *A Guide to Aldeburgh* in 1861), he was the cause of much Aldeburgh-ness in others, including the writers George Meredith, Thomas Hardy, George Gissing, H. G. Wells, and Samuel Butler – many of whom joined Clodd for parties at his home, Strafford House, on Crag Path. The novelist Morley Roberts wrote to Clodd, 'Aldeburgh is the Magnetic Pole, and I perceive some ferric affinity in me to all these others', while Clodd's biographer Joseph McCabe describes Strafford House as 'crammed with memories or ghosts of the great dead who so often shook its windows with laughter'. I'll bet it is. It is a town that punches way above its literary weight, does Aldeburgh, and its many ghosts are nothing like as remote as you might assume. Clodd married his secretary in 1914, a woman forty-seven years younger than him, and Ronald Blythe was able to take tea with her and her companion, a Miss Grant-Duff, in the mid-1950s. As soon as he sat down, Phyllis Clodd ('a bag of bones in a pretty summer dress') told him he was sitting in Thomas Hardy's armchair. A few days after Blythe's visit, Phyllis and Miss Grant-Duff left a note for their gardener telling him not to enter the bedroom, but to call the police. The two had committed suicide together.

As you might hope, in a place with such a literary pedigree, Aldeburgh also has a splendid bookshop, a pirate's treasure chest of happy discoveries. On that first visit the fact of encountering this new seaside was wonderful enough; to find that this seaside had a bookshop was delight beyond measure. I had a warm half-crown in my hand as I walked in (those were the days when one week's pocket money equalled one new paperback – my finances have never been in such perfect accord since); on leaving I held to my heart a copy of Geoffrey Willans's *Down with Skool!*. I read it on the beach. No-one bothered me, save to suggest ice cream. It was a perfect day.

Aldeburgh was not, when I first knew it, smartly cosmopolitan in the way it has now become. The cottages along the High Street were, I think, mostly homes, not tempting little galleries and boutiques, nor let out as five-star holiday cottages; the Cragg sisters still ran the tea room, as they had done since 1949. It still appeared much as it must have done to Henry James: 'the stony beach and the big gales and the cluster of fishermen's huts and the small, wide, short street of decent, homely, shoppy houses.' Yet before shaking one's head too sadly over the *neiges d'antan*, consider this, from the 1861 *Guide*, in which the newly built houses along Crag Path are typified as:

> ... the residences of that fortunate class of people who jostle in the ball room in a London season and live amid the beauties of Nature when she is dressed in gayest hues ... residents in the Town have cause to bless [this] annual influx of smoked-out citizens.

The more things change, the more they stay the same. 'A curious little seaside snuggery' is how that irresistible scoundrel Captain Wragge describes Aldeburgh in *No Name*, as he seeks to lure the heroine, Magdalen Vanstone, to join him there, adding 'I have got the whole house for three guineas a week ... in a fashionable watering-place, such a residence would have been cheap at double the money.' With a wry smile, the writer notes that according to Clodd's 1861 *Guide*, for the 'Julias and Floras, with their Fredericks and Adolphuses, lounging on the shingle,' the summer beach-read was ... *The Woman in White.* I wonder if Wilkie Collins, stomping between hotel and Martello tower the next summer on the same walk on which he would later send Magdalen, spotted his novel in any of their hands.

The rents have changed, but the lure of the place is as strong as ever. Then and now, those taking such cottages are responding to exactly the same charms as I did, and do – the openness above one's head, the human scale of the High Street, the way the backing track of surf on shingle gives you silence and sound both at once, and if it is the weather for that topline to be sequinned, the shimmer there will be in the air and the salt there will be on your lips. It is extraordinary, what we endure in search of a dip. For research purposes only, I – the terrified natator – once again braved the Aldeburgh surf of my childhood. Checking (as I would never have done as a child) that the wind was onshore and the tide coming in, I walked heel-first down the slope of shingle and into the North Sea. A roller walloped me across the chest, then another batted me off yards to the right. The sea tasted the way that blood does, with 'a brutal salt smell, at once clean and rotten,' as Penelope Fitzgerald puts it in *The Bookshop*. The water was the exact grey-green of crab fat, and almost as opaque. When, back home, I stripped to get into the bath, gravel rattled from my swimsuit to the floor. Do we have room for more of the *Suffolk Garland*? I think we do.

Oft, in the fervid blaze of noon,
Sinking beneath the sultry gleam,
I've plunged with Hope's impatient spring,
In thy invigorating stream;

Plung'd – and, while sporting in thy waves,
Derided disappointed Pride;
And with the vile and stagnant bath
Compared thy pure translucent tide.

This from Ann Candler, known as 'the Suffolk Cottager', a self-educated woman poet born in 1740, who worked on most of her poems in the workhouse. She's describing bathing in the River Gipping, but still, wherever we are, we plunge. We can't resist.

Even so, neither the sea nor the beach at Aldeburgh are for the casual bather, and the water is never crowded – yet I was far from the only soul to brave it. Every morning there is a procession of pre-breakfast bathers wrapped in bright robes, padding down the beach to the waves, then padding back into town in search of breakfast. No-one thinks it odd to see an octogenarian sat at a café table, drinking coffee in swimsuit and dressing gown. 'Owlbarrow's like a big open-air bathroom', observes Orlando's daughter, Blanche the kitten, slyly. It says everything about the lure of the sea that we put up with this – the stones, the stinging breakers playing human ping-pong – for that first glorious moment of immersion. When I staggered back up the beach again, I was giggling with pleasure. 'There is no sea like the Aldeburgh sea,' said FitzGerald, another frequent visitor. And afterwards, when you're lying on the beach, skin tightened by the sun and talcum-powdered with salt, flesh gloriously weary from the deep-tissue massage that is the experience of trying to swim in that sea, limbs cushioned on a beach towel laid over those famous pebbles, it feels as if you yourself are evaporating into summer air that the poet George Crabbe described as 'twinkling'.

George Crabbe (1754–1832) is Aldeburgh's poet, famous enough to be mentioned in *No Name*, as if that in itself would locate the place for its readers, but he is so only by default. By birth Crabbe belonged to Slaughden, the hamlet that used to creep along the shingle spit between the end of Aldeburgh's High Street and its Martello tower, like wreckage at the tideline. It must be a sad and difficult thing, to positively hate one's birthplace, but it cannot be said Crabbe was in any way fond of his. His son, the other George, the friend of the heart of Edward FitzGerald, wrote a biography of his famous father in 1834, in which he says:

> Aldborough or as it is more correctly written Aldeburgh was in those days a poor and wretched place with nothing of the elegance and gaiety which have since sprung up about it ... It consisted of two parallel and unpaved streets running between mean and scrambling houses, the abodes of seafaring men pilots and fishers. The range of houses nearest to the sea had suffered so much from repeated invasions of the waves that only a few scattered tenements appeared erect among the desolation.

That range of houses was Slaughden, where Crabbe's father was 'Salt-Master' (a post with the Boards of Customs and Excise), and in the measured language of his grandson, a man of 'imperious temper and violent passions'. In other words, a bully and a drunk and without doubt source material for the poet's creation in *The Borough* of 1810 of the murderous, tormented Peter Grimes. I am sure there were happy souls among the inhabitants of Slaughden, but they have left precious little in the way of a mark: all the images I have been able to find of the place show it as so low-lying it seems to float on the water, its buildings half-buried in great banks of shingle thrown up by the North Sea's dreadful storms. The few inhabitants, blurred and faceless, give the impression of being themselves composed of pebble, salt, and tar. Daniel Defoe noted of Aldeburgh that 'the Sea has of late Years Swallowed up one whole Street.' The sea, along this coast, has a habit of that; other places mashed by the waves include (of course) Dunwich, but even parts of prosperous Southwold have been lost, and of Thorpeness are being threatened even now. William Dutt would describe Slaughden as a 'small, sea-threatened cluster of cottages bordering a primitive quay and grouped around an ancient inn [the Three Mariners] with a huge bone of a whale suspended over its front door'. Crabbe spoke of his father recollecting 'a tremendous spring tide' in 1779, 'when eleven houses here were all demolished and he saw the breakers dash the roofs, curl round the walls, and crush all to ruin.' In the spring of 1953, when the floods were so bad that drowned cows floated down Aldeburgh's High Street, all that remained of Slaughden was finally washed into the sea. And yet this was the place that created George Crabbe, a poet so skilled he could make verse of even the process of atmospheric convection:

> ... the hot and stony beach above,
> Light twinkling streams in bright confusion move ...

Crabbe's poem-portrait of his birthplace, *The Borough*, was read by Benjamin Britten, another native son, in exile in the States in 1941, filling him with nostalgic longing and bringing him and his partner (in music and in life) Peter Pears back to Suffolk and giving Britten the plot and inspiration for his opera *Peter Grimes*. And thus the Aldeburgh Festival, and Snape Maltings concert hall, and Aldeburgh as it is today. More connective tissue. Let us walk.

*

It was not complicated, this walk. It began at Aldeburgh's Martello tower, went back into town along Crag Path, then out of Aldeburgh and straight up the coast. The route turns left just before the Sizewell B nuclear power station, then left again and returns via field paths and byways where the trees meet overhead. But if you do it as Twin and I did, at the end of May, on a day with a sky of blue and clouds puffed as popcorn, and the sea, as Crabbe puts it, keeping 'An equal motion; swelling as it sleeps/Then slowly sinking', you will need sunhat and suncream, especially for that small strip of ankle between trouser-leg and shoe. I sported glowing pink anklets for the next couple of days. Be warned.

Aldeburgh's Martello tower is the largest and most northerly of the chain of such mini-forts built to keep Napoleon at bay, or at least have him think twice before invading. It was built between 1808 and 1810 and was sketched by Turner in 1824. In 1862 we are to imagine Magdalen Vanstone and Captain Wragge making their way here, as a suitable spot for Magdalen to take the Captain into her confidence.

> Slowly and in silence the two walked on until they reached the southern limit of the houses, and entered on a little wilderness of shingle and withered grass – the desolate end of Aldborough, the lonely beginning of Slaughden.

The plot of *No Name* is so complicated it's like literary double-knitting (and in places, it's downright silly), but with it being the follow-up to *The Woman in White,* Wilkie Collins was honour-bound to give his readers their money's worth, and oh, how any writer will sympathise with that. In brief, there is a stolen inheritance, which Magdalen Vanstone determines to retrieve by marrying her cousin, the hideous man-baby Noel Vanstone, as the stolen inheritance is now his. There is much female desperation in the book, which Collins reflects in his high-blown description of the Tower's surroundings:

> ... a lurid streak of sunset glowed red in the dreary heaven, blackened the fringing trees on the far borders of the great inland marsh, and turned its little gleaming water-pools to pools of blood. Nearer to the eye ... the lost little port of Slaughden, with its forlorn wharfs and warehouses of decaying wood, and its few scattered coasting-vessels deserted on the oozy river-shore.

Slaughden has entirely disappeared – as you turn to walk back toward Aldeburgh you will be walking over its ghosts

– to be replaced by the jolly bustle of Aldeburgh's sailing club and dinghy park.

I have a great fondness for dinghy parks, especially the few old decaying boats that always seem to dot their fringes, sails furled after some final outing, and who knows when or where that was, and what plans their owners might have had for more? Instead, here they lie, tilted in the weeds ('on the huh' is the Suffolk dialect phrase), with mould-stained canvas covers no-one has disturbed for years. I also like the way those pools on the marsh have such neat, tucked-in edges, as if the land had been removed from them with a cookie-cutter. Above all I love the sound of halyards *tink*-ing against the dinghies' metal masts. I grew up with that sound, walking through the dinghy park at Waldringfield to the public loos, with their brackish smell and perpetually wet floor (and all the little-girl horror of letting any item of your clothing come into contact with it – nothing but the soles of your feet). At the same age as I first came to know Aldeburgh, I also started 'big school', as it was known, and at the back of our classroom discovered a set of scales that made exactly the same *tink* if one laid a gentle finger on them, and many was the time I did so with a bubble of childhood homesickness in my chest, swelling and sinking like the sea.

By contrast, I have always found Martello towers sinister in the extreme. What happens inside them, to begin with? Then there is no place, as you walk round them, where you are safe from walking into something, as happens to the wretched

Paxton close to this very Martello tower in M. R. James's 'A Warning to the Curious':

> You don't need to be told that he was dead. His tracks showed that he had run along the side of the battery, had turned sharp round the corner of it, and, small doubt of it, must have dashed straight into the open arms of someone who was waiting there. His mouth was full of sand and stones, and his teeth and jaws were broken to bits. I only glanced once at his face.

I was doing the Martello tower start of this walk on my own, and was confiding these thoughts to my phone, with emphasis I am sure, when I realised I was being eyed suspiciously by a pair of fellow walkers, both elderly men.

Fashion in Aldeburgh is a broad church. Dressing gowns are permitted on the High Street; eyebrows lift not at bathing suits that are less vintage than antique. When Orlando goes to the seaside, his landlady, Birdie, accessorises gumboots with flying necklaces and sparkling brooches. The two gentlemen eyeing me askance ('Is she a hands-free, or a care in the community?' their faces asked) were wearing khaki shorts so long and limp they might have been demobbed in them; yet this being Aldeburgh they wore them with cravats about their wrinkled throats and trilbies on their heads, much pinched at the front of the crown. As they passed, they resumed their conversation. Theirs involved the sad deficiencies in avocet parenting.

Time to move on.

So. Back into Aldeburgh proper to collect Twin and Hans, and on to Crag Path, named for the crag sandstone with which it was paved when new in 1861 and apparently then 'brightly orange in the sunshine'. Brightwell Swale, that empty heathland to the east of Ipswich, if it is haunted by anything, should be haunted by the flip-flopping marine ghosts of the Pliocene, beating their tails through the bracken. There are places where the orange-red crag of which the Swale is composed rears its way free of the turf, where shells and whole, flinty-black shark teeth, if you are lucky, can be freed from the shaley crag with nothing more powerful than a finger, and the whole of it as crude a colour as sand from a builder's merchant. All that is now under your feet, yards from the seas where those sharks once swam, while the palette of colour surrounding you today is that of the blues and pinks and creams and greens and well-bred mauves and yellows of the houses on Crag Path. Here is Strafford House. Here is the lookout tower once associated with Laurens van der Post, who like so many literary fossils now no longer bears close scrutiny. Here is Clare Cottage, where FitzGerald lodged. Here Crag Path has a gap, like a jaw that has lost a tooth, and peering through the gap from King Street is the house where Patricia Highsmith sat and fretted over her married mistress, who was up in London and fretting over Highsmith not at all. Here is the north lookout tower, also in *No Name*, and the yard of the Cross Keys pub; and now the fishermen's tar-black sheds begin, and there is the RNLI station, and shortly after that the house where Ruth Rendell made a home. And now the Jubilee Hall. At this point you should also be marvelling, if you make this walk in May, at the colours of the red valerian, which may be red, but may also be crimson, or rose pink, or white, all higgled together and flowering gloriously in what is apparently nothing but pebble with a top coat of sand. (Later in the year, you would be gasping at Aldeburgh's hollyhocks.) Twin took in a lungful of ozone and sunlight, then gave a cry, pointing above her head: 'Look up there!'

Ah yes. Aldeburgh's famous swifts. It is always good to see a swift; even better to have them nest under your eaves, in which case you must never, ever destroy their nests while they are away, or woe betide you.

> Oh, swift-wing'd bird of sunny skies
> And gentle zephyrs, how I prize,
> Lov'd, vagrant swallow, thy return
> From thy far distant long sojourn!

wrote Laetitia Jermyn, pioneering woman entomologist and wife to James Ford, creator of the first *Suffolk Garland*. There Laetitia's swifts were, twisting and diving overhead, and never ceasing to natter to each other as they did so. Given the speed at which they loop and turn you do wonder if the noise might be shouts of warning, like the horns in frenzied traffic. So much about these birds was a mystery for so long.

'Our Summer Friends the Swallows,' Defoe calls them, breaking out of his reportage voice to mention their prevalence 'nowhere so much as on this Eastern coast.' At different times swallows (and swifts, and house martins – Merlin informed us we had all three performing acrobatics above us) were thought to be without feet, so rarely did they settle. They can in fact go as long as ten months on the wing, and for centuries their disappearance at the end of summer was accounted for by the belief that after they had disappeared out to sea they dived down and spent the winter underwater, twisting and hunting just as they did in the air. We know now – back over the Dogger Bank they go, and turn south. The largest swallow might reach 10 inches long and weigh a little over a couple of ounces. End to end, it would take 6,300 of them to stretch a single mile, and they might fly 8,000 miles (13,000 kilometres) in one migration. For Crabbe, their freedom was everything he longed for:

> As on their neighbouring beach yon swallows stand,
> And wait for favoring winds to leave the land;
> While still for flight the ready wing is spread:
> So waited I the favouring hour, and fled ...

We continued – past the war memorial and on to the Moot Hall, where in 1956 Ronald Blythe once spent the night as history's most unlikely security guard to an exhibition of Jean-François Millet's drawings, curated for the Aldeburgh

Festival by Sir Kenneth Clark, no less. One of these, I hope and like to think, might have been a drawing for Millet's painting *The Angelus*, completed in 1857–9. Robert Louis Stevenson could have known Millet through his friend the artist Wyatt Eaton, who had a studio in Paris near Millet's, and when Stevenson came to describe the labourers he saw in a field in France on a walk of his own, I think he had Millet's masterpiece in his head: 'An immense shadow fills the plain; these people stand in it up to their shoulders; and their heads, as they stoop over their work and rise again, are relieved from time to time against the golden sky.' In the same festival of 1956, E. M. Forster was lecturing in the Jubilee Hall. You see what I mean about Aldeburgh punching above its weight?

You know you are out of Aldeburgh proper when the famous House in the Clouds pops out of the trees ahead of you, pinpointing the time-slip resort of Thorpeness, along with the grey concrete behemoth and white bubble of Sizewell B (the latter, to me, instantly suggestive of a mushroom cloud), and on the horizon some other structure nastily reminiscent of H. G. Wells's *The War of the Worlds*. By now, we were also within reach of the 'Scallop', Maggi Hambling's oddly flirtatious sculpture, and far enough from Aldeburgh itself, between the months of May to September, to be allowed to release Hans off his lead. If you have a Hans of your own with you, you can do the same, in which case I can promise you the first thing he or she will do is race madly across the shingle, tail and ears bouncing in polyphonic counterpoint, charge round and round the Scallop, then wee on it. The Scallop may quote Peter Grimes, it may commemorate Benjamin Britten; it belongs to the dogs.

Twin is a great collector of interesting stones, as was Ouida too, apparently. In her 1957 biography of the writer, Monica Stirling reports that sometimes on her walks Ouida 'would pick up a stone lying by the wayside, take it home, and make a sort of pet of it, saying it was lonely and uncared for.' We have to feel our way into everything, we writers. Nothing is safe. Although when on this walk I found a pebble that had been inscribed in thick black marker 'Put me back!', I did. By this point the noise of the sea was all about us, 'a sea on its cosmic leash', as Blythe described it from his winter lodgings in Thorpeness, 'rushing at me then pulled back'. There were roofs coming into view, and garden hedges scrambling down to the beach, and on all of them the unabashed magenta of the dog rose.

The dog rose is the county flower of Hampshire, but surely it should be that of Suffolk. You see it everywhere around Thorpeness, scrambling over fences and climbing up trees. It puts those over-bred, heavy-headed, toilet-paper-coloured cultivars to shame, both with its spirit and the purity of its sweet scent. This is how the roses smelled in Eden. They mark the spot where it is time to head inland, up a lane between the houses, and into Thorpeness itself.

*

It would be very easy to mock Thorpeness, and mocked it has been, for sure. Ronald Blythe described it as 'everything a colonialist on furlough might need'. It's a place inspired by a dream of an England that never existed, as if 1914 and everything afterwards never happened, an Edwardian idyll created completely falsely to share that dream for one week of the year with those others (and only those others) who might be expected to yearn for it. The houses facing the beach at Thorpeness are eclectic enough – one a sort of beach hut on steroids, one crazily modernist, another a gentleman's residence with sunrooms grafted on to all three of its storeys – but they are nothing compared to the oddity of Thorpeness itself, with its half-timbered Tudorbethan villas and its village green and above all its Meare, which is the size of a lake but nowhere deeper than a metre. One rich man, Glencairn Stuart Ogilvie, created Thorpeness in 1910, building up what had been a tiny hamlet with a reputation for smuggling into a resort upon which perhaps he hoped the sun truly would never set. It has a golf club, tennis courts, a swimming pool, and once upon a time its own railway station as well. It has almshouses too, so that those who loved Thorpeness as children might grow old there and never have to return to the outside world at all. This is either profoundly sad or deeply unsettling once you know that J. M. Barrie of *Peter Pan* fame was an Ogilvie family friend much involved in the creation of the Meare in particular, so that children of the right sort (Thorpeness was never aimed at the working class: let them go down the coast to Clacton or Margate) could spend a little time messing about in boats in the right and proper fashion, in water shallow enough for them to be unlikely to drown in it. (I *loathe* Peter Pan, the heartless little freak – not so much the boy who never grew up as the boy who never wanted to, if we are talking man-babies: spiritual father to Oskar in Günter Grass's *The Tin Drum*.) Yes, it would be easy to mock, as with the architecture of the beach houses – but as with them, what is one thing to the outsider is quite another to those living within it. Think how wonderful it would be for every floor of your house to be flooded with the light of the sea; think how your inner child would love to take a boat out on the Meare, to Crusoe's Island or The Dragon's Den, in water shallow enough to be able to *keep that toe on the bottom*, and to stroll home across a village green complete with ducks and a donkey in a hat. I had always thought of Thorpeness as being Aldeburgh's poor relation, a sort of spinster cousin, if you like; I was completely wrong. Thorpeness is charming. It has a winning air of determination – all England could be like this, it seems to say, if only you would *try*. It reminded me of the nervy optimism of the mother in Hitchcock's *Shadow of a Doubt*, all the while overlaid by the suspicion that one is about to walk into Patrick McGoohan from *The Prisoner*. Also, it has a tea room overlooking the Meare, and we needed sustenance. Two middle-aged ladies and small dog, restoring ourselves with coffee and sticky buns. 'How long is this walk?' asked Twin, who had one early morning online meeting under her belt already and another hovering over her late afternoon.

'Long,' said I. 'The longest in the book. Ten miles. Ten or twelve.'

Twin glanced down at Hans, who was trying to engage a poodle under the next table in conversation. 'I am not sure he can walk for that long,' she said, then added, 'I do not know if I can, either.'

Thorpeness marks where you leave the beach via 'The Sanctuary' and shift your walk to the clifftop. The wind is gentler up here: the sound of the sea too, in the ears no louder than it is in a shell. As we walked, the shadows of clouds shoaled across the water, marbling grey with grey; the bright tips of the waves turned and turned; seagulls drifted and lingered in that peculiar flight as if they had a wire through their breast holding them up, and two more controlling their wings. Reassuring signs, bumblebee yellow and black, told us we were on the coast path; others, more mysterious, spoke of 'Warden's Hall'. We walked past the spikiest hawthorn I have ever seen, worse than anything any medieval artist ever dreamed up for Christ's crown of thorns, and then past romping honeysuckle the exact pink and yellow of old-fashioned rhubarb-and-custard boiled sweets. Now we were in a sort of covered lane: a shoulder-height wall to our left, surprisingly thick and covered in a skin of ancient concrete, and to our right, angled over the path, a sloping growth of scrubby trees, battered backwards by the wind. It took a while to puzzle out the presence of the wall, but we did in the end – or I think we did. It was that skin of concrete, and the wall's resemblance thereby to the look of the pillboxes that still dot Suffolk's fields. 'I think it must be from the war,' said Twin, and of course she was right. The events of 1914 did happen, as did those of 1939; the wall was what the troops defending the English coast would have stood behind, to fire upon the invaders coming from occupied France. It was the reflection, across the mirror of the North Sea, of the beach defences in Normandy. Hard now to understand the misgiving with which those flat lands across the North Sea were once held, but they were – there were the Dutch and their prodigious navy in the seventeenth century, the French under Napoleon (hence the Martello towers), and in 1925, when M. R. James wrote 'A Warning to the Curious', Paxton's crime is that he removes from its burial place one of three holy crowns buried 'near by the coast to keep the Germans from landing'. 'Ah,' says Paxton's informant, 'I can see you don't believe that. But I tell you, if it hadn't 'ave been for one of them 'oly crowns bein' there still, them Germans would a landed here time and again, they would. Landed with their ships, and killed man, woman and child in their beds.' The next Great Heathen Army, in other words. The Suffolk coast does not forget. But while walls remain, they may lose their purpose, and paths that once bore marching feet now had only Twin and I, a pair of *rambleuses*, puzzling our way along, and if we had writerly company, it was Adam Dalgliesh, eyeing Sizewell B and wondering if 'this great hulk would one day yield to the sea, like the wave-smashed concrete from the last war.'

A strange little bridge ran above our heads, over the path, and down to the shore. This, we decided, must be part of Sizewall Hall, once the Ogilvie family home. Then the trees and wall and scrub all stopped at once, and instead there was a wide green heath, a sky of Baltic blue. 'Here you are down at Aldeburgh,' wrote Hardy to Clodd, 'enjoying the sensation of having nothing but sea between you and the North Pole.' Clodd, 'fine and brave pagan that he was,' as his biographer described him, had his ashes scattered into that sea. I hope whoever was in charge of doing so brought Phyllis Clodd's ashes out there as well, to mingle with her husband's after so long, but perhaps she chose to be buried with the companion with whom she also chose to meet Death. I was musing on who Clodd's spirit might be mixing with down there – sailors from the Battle of Solebay? Dunwich merchants, swept from their beds? – when Twin, with an eye to Hans, still trotting gamely along beside us despite his heartbreak over the poodle, pointed out that this was the Sizewell Gap, so-called, where we were to change direction once more.

The Sizewell Gap is a fine straight road, and even has a pavement (you know how rare those are in the Suffolk countryside). Remembering the scarred fields, the naked earth, the roadworks of the taxi ride to Blythburgh, I assumed it must be a leftover, a sop to the locals, from the period when Sizewell B was being built, but no – there it is on Bryant's map of Suffolk of 1824. It would take us into Leiston, if we wished, but we did not. There was a road off to the left, Sizewell Hall Road, such as walkers dream of, untarmacked, with muddy sides, running straight between trees that were thick with green, dappled with shadow, and resonant with birdsong. Merlin could barely keep up. A dunnock, a whitethroat, a garden warbler; a redstart, a chaffinch, a meadow pipit, a collared dove, a sedge warbler; the endless wood pigeons and then far off, a cuckoo – the first I had heard in years. A side effect of Merlin-ing is that you find yourself starting to recognise birdsongs almost as fast as it does: that furious if tuneful cacophony is a wren. That pleasing warble, a dunnock. You not only hear this new and otherwise invisible world; you start to learn its languages, too. It is as if you have acquired a new sense on top of the normal five, as if through your ears you can see. We stopped only to scoop Hans out of the way as a Post Office van drove past. Some lucky soul lives out here, we thought, and yes, there was the odd roof or gable just visible through the trees, and as we followed our noses down one path then the next, they performed those disconcerting castling moves where it was as if they were moving with us, keeping pace on their side of the fields. Above one such field a lark was singing, invisible against the sky. The nineteenth-century journo William Cobbett spent most of his time in Suffolk, in his *Rural Rides* of 1830, fulminating against the 'Pittites' among the local gentry, or patting him himself on the back for the reception given to his public talks, but outside Ipswich, a skylark stops him in his tracks:

> A lark, very near to me in a ploughed field, rose from the ground, and was saluting the sun with his delightful song. He was got about as high as the dome of St. Paul's, having me for a motionless and admiring auditor, when the hen started up from nearly the same spot whence the cock had risen, flew up and passed close by him. I could not hear what she said; but supposed that she must have given him a pretty smart reprimand; for down she came upon the ground, and he, ceasing to sing, took a twirl in the air and came down after her. Others have, I dare say, seen this a thousand times over; but I never observed it before.

But there was even better to come. Two children – a boy and a girl – bounced past us on pushbikes, calling back over their shoulders to apologise for their speed, but we were now on a path wide enough and hard enough and dry enough to race your sibling on it, so who could blame them? It was perfect Suffolk dirt, slightly tinged with red, and as fine as if milled. Hans's snowy whiteness was being overlaid with pink. We came to a place where the track branched one way into a field, leaving a triangular patch of mounded green, of low trees and tall bushes, and standing a little away from it, stooped in a posture of unusual attention, there was a man. He spotted us. 'Are you interested in birds?' he asked. I flourished my phone. 'Oh, you have Merlin,' he said, at once. He pointed to the bosky triangle. 'That,' he said, 'is a nightingale,' and it was.

You may think you have heard birdsong, but until you have heard a nightingale singing in the wild you have not. If the best blackbird-singer on the planet was to be trained by Joan Sutherland, it might get close. The fullness, the roundness, the clarity ... The laughter as it sang. The variety of its song. Twin and I were open-mouthed, almost with disbelief, that this moment had been gifted to us. On it went, with a little movement in the leaves as it hopped from one branch to the next. Finally, a pale flash on one topmost branch, a dip of a gingerish wing, and it was gone. 'It's late in the year for him to be singing in the day,' our new friend commented. Not a man in need of Merlin, clearly. He turned to us. 'You seen a couple of kids on bikes come this way?'

The honeysuckle in the hedges now had gorse supporting it, gorse in full flower, of the same bumblebee yellow as the earlier signs. The sun was pouring more and more heat down onto us, the paths becoming narrower. I had the feeling perhaps only another redhead will recognise, of being almost tipsy with sunlight. The dog roses had reappeared. We crossed the B1353 without even the sound of traffic, walked on, and reached the North Warren Nature Reserve, where there was another pair of walkers, the only others we had seen: a man and woman, he with binoculars about his neck. We exchanged hellos, as walkers must. 'There's a marsh harrier over there,' the man said, pointing out across a reedbed on the right and lifting his binoculars as proof, but if there was, we couldn't see it, nor Merlin hear it, and of course for it to count, Merlin has to hear it too. For all that we must have walked a good 9 miles (15 kilometres) by this point, our hairpin route meant that Thorpeness was again within striking distance to the east. The husband and wife were walking back there, they said. Twin and I pondered. She said her presence wasn't a necessity at the meeting that afternoon, but her demeanour as she said it didn't match her words. She would have fretted had she missed it. We looked at Hans. Hans lay down with his muzzle on his paws and his eyebrows twitching as he looked back at each of us in turn: *please*, those eyebrows said, *please don't make me explain this to you both again*. Decision made. Twin would go back to Thorpeness with Hans; I would walk back to Aldeburgh on my own.

I am no Cheryl Strayed. My life would have had to disintegrate beyond recognition for me to do as she did and decide to fix it by walking 1,100 miles (1,800 kilometres) of the Pacific Crest Trail – of *any* trail – on my own. I am not one for sleeping under canvas, either. I used to joke to my girlfriends that if I woke and couldn't immediately see a mirror and an electric socket I would start to hyperventilate, and although they never knew it, it was only a joke because they didn't believe me. I had at most a couple of miles to walk on my own down gentle country lanes, and I was astonished at how apprehensive I felt. In London I walk on my own all the time, getting up from my laptop to put some of those necessary moments of distance between me and whatever I am working on; striding round the Isle of Dogs while I put sentences through their paces in my head. Sometimes, yes, at night, I walk with my house keys protruding between my fingers in the city girl's version of Wolverine's claws, scanning my surroundings and with my senses on as high an alert as any of my long-ago ancestors nervously walking the grasslands; but walking in the city and walking in the country are not the same, not at all. In the city there are other people all around you, all the time; here there were not. I looked down the lane ahead, as if to judge its potential for bad endings. 'You live in the country, you spend every minute of the day surrounded by a vast emptiness ... But you never think for a minute that you might become part of it,' as unwilling investigator Susan Ryeland puts it in *Moonflower Murders*. The last time I had walked in the country on my own, I was not on my own, either: I would have been walking with Fergus, our wolfhound, loping along beside me. To be honest Fergus was so easy-going I am not sure how he would have reacted to an outright threat, but one look at him, his great wolf's head at the level of my waist, and his Minotaur shoulders, and any likely threat would have thought better of it and slunk away. And a dog gives one a reason for walking: it's obvious why you are out there. While walking for the sake of walking, as

Patricia Highsmith's Sydney Bartleby would no doubt have agreed, is difficult to explain; it is transgressive behaviour that attracts further transgressive behaviour in turn. I thought of my mother's mother, never leaving the house without making up some little package of nothing to carry with her, to give her a reason for doing so. I felt as if to walk on my own as a woman here would be somehow breaking the rules, and we all know what happens to women who do that.

Fear, says Cheryl Strayed, is born of the story we tell ourselves. Tell yourself a different story, said I to myself, one where you are perfectly safe, where this small section of walk done on your own is a privilege, a special experience, an unexpected coda. Put down that package of nothing. Hit the road.

The trees closed over me. The birds sang. Chaffinch, Merlin informed me. There was a ditch beside the road full of yellow flag iris, a hut or maybe a hide up ahead with a big red spray-painted heart by its door, topped and tailed by a 'YOU' and a 'ME', and then, this being 2025, 'TRANS RIGHTS' in white around the corner from the door, and the three-horned trans symbol. The trees began to space themselves out. Over the field to my right was a house big enough for me to remember it as being on the outskirts of Aldeburgh, then the end of the path, where the vista through the trees reached its vanishing point, was unmistakably underlined by pavement. And there were three lads, walkers, with rucksacks and water bottles, just setting out. I stood back to let them pass. 'Thanks,' they said. A message from Twin: she'd taken her meeting online, back at the café in Thorpeness, and was on her way home by bus. There was one more short walk I had to take, to Wentworth Street, then I too would be done.

In *No Name*, the house in Aldeburgh taken by Captain Wragge is called North Shingles. There is no North Shingles in Aldeburgh, but there is a North House, close by the hotel where Wilkie Collins stayed. At dawn, on the morning of her wedding to Noel Vanstone, which is to be at the church of St Peter and St Paul, Magdalen sits at its window looking out to sea, and so torn in heart and mind is she that she sits with a bottle of laudanum beside her, ready to take her own life rather than marry. There is the sea before her, there is that high horizon, there a line of vessels heading home.

> She resolved to end the struggle by setting her life or death on the hazard of a chance.
>
> On what chance? ...
>
> The sea showed it to her. For one half-hour to come she determined to wait there and count the vessels as

> they went by. If in that time an even number passed her, the sign given should be a sign to live. If the uneven number prevailed, the end should be Death.

The first ship passes by. Then a second. Then a third. Wilkie Collins is doing something incredibly modern here: the ships pass by on the horizon before Magdalen's eyes, the word 'ship' moves across the page before the reader's eyes, with us as tense for the arrival of the next as Wilkie's heroine. It's something akin to concrete verse – you might call it 'animated prose' perhaps. There's a fourth, 'slower than the rest, larger than the rest, further off in the mist than the rest.' The minutes are ticking past. The fifth ship appears. You wait and wait and *wait* for the sixth. It arrives, but so does a seventh. It is the most nerve-wracking piece of Victorian fiction I have ever encountered. As Victorian fiction, it is quite extraordinary.

> ... nothing followed in the wake of the seventh ship. The minute-hand of the watch moved on half-way to thirty, and still the white heaving sea was a misty blank. Without moving her head from the window, she took the poison in one hand, and raised the watch in the other. As the quick seconds counted each other out, her eyes, as quick as they, looked from the watch to the sea, from the sea to the watch – looked for the last time at the sea – and saw the EIGHTH ship.

The fictitious ship moves along the horizon, the word 'ship' moves along the line of text. Writers always approach an ending with caution, but in a book about walking and writing and thinking and Suffolk, I don't think I can do better than that.

FIN

London, Bury, Aldeburgh, Brooklyn
2025

The Writers

Below is a *bonne bouche* of pocket-size biographies for the most significant Suffolk writers featured in this book. Names in bold show where one writer's life crossed with another, and where they too have an entry.

Adrian Bell

Few before him, and very few since, have created as much good writing out of the seemingly wholly unliterary occupation of farming as Bell (1901–80). His Suffolk trilogy – *Corduroy*, *Silver Ley*, and *The Cherry Tree* – records a world that almost disappeared with the Second World War, and does so with great affection but without sentimentality; back-to-the-land writing by one who lived it. Bell wrote more than twenty books in all; at the suggestion (again) of his father, he also became the first setter of crossword clues for *The Times*, notching up a tally of more than 5,000 puzzles.

James Bird

Born in the village of Earl Stonham in 1788, Bird worked as a miller in Yoxford until about 1819, when he opened a stationer's shop instead, which supported him and his family of sixteen children until his death in 1839. Largely self-taught, he was contributing poems to the *Suffolk Chronicle* as a teenager. At its greatest, his reputation was being compared to that of **Robert Bloomfield**. He also wrote two plays, one of which, *The Smuggler's Daughter*, was produced at Sadler's Wells. Knowing he was dying, he wrote 'A Word at Parting with the Year 1838', which details with wry good humour all the ailments he had endured in the previous twelve months, including influenza that 'curled me up just like a shrimp.'

Robert Bloomfield

Bloomfield's mother was the village schoolmistress, otherwise he might have remained as unlettered as many another Suffolk child in the eighteenth century. Born in 1766 and sent to London in 1781 in to learn shoemaking with his brother, he took to reading *The London Magazine* to his fellow apprentices, which at the time had a poetry section. Thus, the poet was born.

Bloomfield composed his poems in his head, working over and memorising scores of lines at a time. He was admired by John Constable, who used Bloomfield's most famous poem, *The Farmer's Boy*, for the titles of two of his paintings, and by

Robert Southey, later Poet Laureate, and in the early 1800s enjoyed notable success. But his publishers went bankrupt in 1812, his eyesight failed, and when he died in 1823 it was in great want and unhappiness. His books and manuscripts had all to be sold to give him a funeral.

James Blyth

Blyth was born as Henry James Catling Clabburn in Norwich in 1864, changing his name in 1898 after a scandalous divorce in which both he and his wife sued each other for adultery. A decided literary oddity, Blyth was to abandon a career as a solicitor to write, and hoped to create a 'Daneshire' and a reputation for himself to match that of Thomas Hardy and 'Wessex'. He used the history of his own wildly dysfunctional family for his novel *Celibate Sarah*; but is best known (insofar as he is at all) for his speculative fiction, which gave him full scope to air his xenophobia ('jeering Prussian sausage-munchers' being a particularly eyebrow-raising phrase). He died in 1933.

Ronald Blythe

Ronald Blythe, man of letters, writer of *Akenfield* and *The Time by the Sea* and much else, belongs to Suffolk as Emily Brontë does to Yorkshire. He was both product and chronicler of the county, as Suffolk as a tractor, a reedbed, or an oak. Born in 1922, a descendant of generations of Suffolk farmers and farmhands, Blythe (who left school at fourteen and was largely self-educated) was working as a librarian in Colchester when a meeting with John Nash's wife Christine brought him into the Nash's circle of East Anglian writers and artists. Although he wanted to be an artist himself, surely this self-described 'watcher and listener' was never meant to be anything other than a writer, and the chronicler of Suffolk as it moved from its centuries-old rural character into the twentieth and twenty-first centuries.

Blythe inherited Bottengoms Farm, in Wormingford on the Suffolk/Essex border, from Nash and lived there until his own death at the age of 100 in 2023. His meditations – on rural life, on the turnings of the year, on ageing, on everything – appeared in his 'Word from Wormingford' column in the *Church Times* for twenty-five years and were published in several books of essays. A splendid biography by Ian Collins was published in 2024.

Ann Candler

Few of Ann Candler's poems give any hint of the hardship and tragedy of her life. Born Ann More in Yoxford in 1740, she had family connections to both Woodbridge and Ipswich, while her husband came from the village of Sproughton. But the marriage was not a happy one – her husband, who was a drinker, left Ann when she was pregnant with their first child, initiating a pattern of desertion that was to continue throughout their married life. By 1777, Ann and four of their six children were in the workhouse. She was in the workhouse again in March 1781, at Tattingstone near Ipswich, where she gave birth to twin sons, and where both infants died. Ann was still there a year later when she wrote a poem beginning 'How many years are past and gone,/How altered I appear!' In 1783 her husband joined her in the workhouse himself, but six months later he left and she never saw him again. 'All I can urge to extenuate, or palliate my folly is, that he was my husband, and the father of my children, and that my affection for him was unbounded,' she wrote in 1801, in a long autobiographical note.

Ann had taught herself to read and write in girlhood. Her first poem was published in 1785, in the *Ipswich Journal*; the support of Elizabeth Cobbold, of the wealthy local brewing family, led to the publication of Candler's *Poetical Attempts* in 1803 (now available online). By this time Ann, 'the Suffolk Cottager' poet, as she had become known, was living near her married daughter at Copdock, at long last under her own roof. She died in 1814.

Edward Clodd

A man with a happy genius for friendship, Clodd (1840–1930) lived in Aldeburgh almost all his adult life. His first marriage, to Eliza Garman in 1862, produced eight children;

his second was to his secretary, Phyllis Maud Rope, who was forty-seven years his junior. Over the years his reputation as a folklorist, anthropologist, and host lured almost every notable literary figure of the day to his house in Aldeburgh – a one-man Aldeburgh Festival, if you like. His charming guidebook is available online – some enterprising Aldeburghian needs to reprint it.

William Cobbett

Journalist, politician, farmer, political prisoner, American exile, and all-round pain in the establishment backside, Cobbett (1763–1835) was born at Farnham in Surrey. *Rural Rides*, a survey of sorts of the state of the nation brought him to Suffolk in the winter of 1821, and he was back again in the spring of 1830. He was delighted by the 'hearty welcome' he received from the Suffolk farmers, which, given Cobbett's inability to back down from any kind of fight whatsoever, was just as well. Said he, 'I have always found Suffolk farmers great boasters of their superiority over others; and I must say that it is not without reason.'

Henry Cockton

Born in London in 1807, an apprenticeship as a draper may have brought Cockton to Bury St Edmunds, where at the age of thirty he married Anne, daughter of Eleanor Howe, the landlady of The Seven Stars. The marriage produced a daughter and a son, and in 1841 *The Life and Adventures of Valentine Vox,* which begins in a town very like Bury, and in a pub very like that (one imagines) run by Henry's mother-in-law. The novel was a success, with some 400,000 copies published over the next fifty years (it was last in print in 1920), but what little the author saw of the profits were soon lost: one of his publishers collapsed; then he stood surety for a brother, who hot-footed it to Australia; then Cockton decided he would go into the malting business, about which he knew nothing, with predictable results. His marriage suffered, it seems he and wife separated, and his last novels are much less high-spirited and happy than his first; although long after Cockton's death in 1853, his writing was singled out by no less an authority than Robertson Davies, one of the great men of Canadian letters. A late work is also set in Suffolk: *Lady Felicia* (1852), a Cinderella story in reverse in which a shop assistant is wed by a titled lady, begins 'In the celebrated borough of Sudbury ...'

Wilkie Collins

Wilkie Collins (1824–89) can lay claim to having invented both the mystery novel and (with Dickens and Edgar Allan Poe) the character of the professional detective. (Fittingly, **P. D. James** was a great admirer.) *No Name* is the second in the incredible run of works Collins produced in the 1860s, topped and tailed by *The Woman in White* and *The Moonstone*. It's high praise to say it is *almost* as good as either of them, and it is particularly pleasing that after the horror of her marriage, Magdalen finds happiness ever after with an Aldeburgh sea captain.

Collins was meant to follow in his father's footsteps as an artist, and when he refused that path, to become a lawyer. But a bully at school in Highbury had forced the teenage Collins to come up with a story a night *or else*, and that was that. Intriguingly, William Collins, Wilkie's father, was in correspondence with Bernard Barton, Woodbridge's 'Quaker poet'.

George Crabbe

Crabbe (1754–1832) was attempting and failing to make a living as a poet in London when out of desperation he contacted the philosopher Edmund Burke, who introduced Crabbe to the London literati (including Dr Johnson, one of *The Village*'s first readers) and secured for Crabbe the post of chaplain to the Duke of Rutland, whose patronage of the poet continued for years.

Crabbe's poetry would come to be admired by Byron, by Sir Walter Scott, by Jane Austen, by Robert Southey, by Tennyson, and by Wordsworth, yet on a visit to London he was surprised by the adulation with which he was received. 'In my own village,' he was to observe mildly, 'They think nothing of me.' He might have been thinking of Slaughden, of

Aldeburgh, of Parham, or of Great Glemham, all in Suffolk and all of which could lay claim to him being 'theirs' at one time or another. There can be many such villages in a writer's life.

Daniel Defoe

In his lifetime, Defoe's *Tour Thro' the Whole Island of Great Britain* ... was his most successful work after *Robinson Crusoe.* Defoe (1660–1731) is often described as having invented modern journalism, but for much of his professional life he also worked as a merchant, in England and on the Continent. His *Tour* of 1724–7 was supplemented by his earlier travels (he says he first knew Ipswich in 1668, for example). It is chatty and discursive and interested in everything: from the Suffolk trade in turkeys, to the state of Suffolk shipbuilding, to the 'chamber of rarities' belonging to a Mr White of Bury St Edmunds, with 'things very curious in it, as particularly a sea-horse carefully preserved, and perfect in all its parts; [and] two Roman urns full of ashes of human bodies'.

Charles Dickens

Dickens (1812–70) had much Suffolk experience at his disposal as a writer. He used Blundeston in north Suffolk as David Copperfield's birthplace; the storm that drowns both Steerforth and Ham at the end of that same book is a North

Sea storm; and the beach upon which their bodies are washed up is a Suffolk beach. Satis House, near Saxmundham, where Dickens was a guest, has been put forward as the inspiration for Miss Havisham's decaying mansion of the same name in *Great Expectations*. On a lighter note, Mr Pickwick of *The Pickwick Papers* encounters a local celebrity, a lady poet, Mrs Leo Hunter, who bears similarities to Elizabeth Cobbold (she who was the patron of **Ann Candler**). The fictitious Mrs Hunter is the author of 'Ode to a Dying Frog':

> Can I view thee panting, lying
> On thy stomach, without sighing;
> Can I unmoved see thee dying
> On a log
> Expiring frog!

'Beautiful! exclaims Mr Pickwick.

William Dowsing

Dowsing (1596–1668) rose with his patron the 2nd Earl of Manchester in the army of the Eastern Association during the English Civil War. Thank heaven the career of 'Smasher Dowsing' came to an end when Manchester got on the wrong side of Oliver Cromwell and was dismissed. Dowsing's *Journal* (available online at Internet Archive) records with unforgivable glee his predations against churches throughout East Anglia, either in person or through a small army of assistants. To add insult to injury he then charged each church for his attentions.

William Alfred Dutt

Dutt (1870–1939) was a writer and naturalist born at Ditchingham in Norfolk: a specialist on all aspects of East Anglian life and folklore, and a supporter of Alfred Watkins's theory of ley lines. He was also a biographer of George Borrow (1803–81), the writer of *Lavengro* and *Romany Rye* and so-called 'walking lord of gipsy lore'. Many of Dutt's works are available online; they are also to be found in many a second-hand bookshop.

Celia Fiennes

Famous as being one of the earliest woman travellers, Fiennes rode around England between 1684 and 1712 or so 'to regain my health', so she said, and on the way created the genre of cultural and economic tourism taken up by **Daniel Defoe** in the 1720s. She wrote her memoirs for family reading in 1702. They sometimes give the impression that Celia travelled on her own, but as a granddaughter of the 1st Viscount Saye and Sele she was always accompanied by at least a servant or two. She was nonetheless highly unusual for her time, both for the doors her name opened to her (she was a great visitor of grand country houses) and the tartness of her observations once she had passed through them. Fiennes died in Hackney in 1741 at the age of seventy-nine; today the 1888 edition of her travels, *Through England on a Side Saddle*, is available online. She was impressed by Suffolk's markets, its butter, its spinners and knitters, and by the country house Euston Hall, but warned against Suffolk's 'long miles', its 'many dissenters', and its winds: 'in ye winter, not well to be endured'.

George Ewart Evans

Evans (1909–88), a folklorist and essayist, and a Welshman by birth, came to live in Suffolk in 1947 after serving in the Second World War. Like **Ronald Blythe**, he was moved to investigate and to record a way of life he saw disappearing all around him, in particular with the passing of the farmers and farmhands from the generation before the First World War. His *Ask the Fellows Who Cut the Hay* came out in 1956 and was the first in a run of more than a dozen books recording oral history and rural traditions and ways of life.

Evans was also a praiseworthily early example of the house-husband: as a writer in Blaxhall he was the stay-at-home parent, while his wife ran the village school.

Edward FitzGerald

There is little I can say of FitzGerald (1809–83) other than advise that you read him; the more you read him, the better he gets. **Clement King Shorter**, one of the founders of the Omar Khayyam Club, wrote that:

> It is generally agreed that FitzGerald, a nineteenth-century pagan, always reverently questioning the mystery of existence, superadded his own personal thoughts and feelings to the verses of the old Persian singer. In doing this he touched deeply a certain aspect of the second half of the nineteenth century and founded a cult. FitzGerald's verses, however, have been ardently admired by many who are far from accepting their pessimist view of life.

Ronald Blythe was presented with a copy of the *Rubaiyat* as a goodbye gift by a West Country jeweller with whom he had enjoyed a summer fling; he was a lifelong admirer of FitzGerald from then on. Robert Bernard Martin's biography of FitzGerald is well worth exploring too.

James Ford

Ford (1799–1850) was another of that splendid breed, the English antiquary-cum-churchman, and the compiler of the first *Suffolk Garland*, of 1818, in which 'our County Readers are here presented with some select specimens of their native Bards, and provincial Rhymers'. You can find it now online at HathiTrust. Ford was described as 'an ardent bibliophile', but pompous with it, which is exactly the personality that comes across from his Preface to the *Garland*.

In 1830 Ford married the pioneering entomologist Laetitia Jermyn, who with the encouragement of her neighbour William Kirby, had published *The Butterfly Collector's Vade Mecum* in 1824. Kirby was the grandson of the topographer **John Kirby** – it's a small world, Suffolk.

Esther Freud

Walberswick is just as much a haunt of artist and writers as it was in **M. R. James**'s day; Esther Freud is one among them. She's perhaps best known for the biographical *Hideous Kinky*; in *The Sea House* (2003) there is an element of family history again, in the refugee character of the protagonist, Max, plus any number of Suffolk locations that hide their identities under assumed names but remain unmistakable for all that. There is creative struggle, too, part healed by the landscape in which it plays out, part exacerbated by it. The same push-and-pull within the same Suffolk setting is also there in *Mr Mac and Me* (2014).

John Glyde

Historian, radical thinker, and bookseller, Glyde was born in Ipswich in 1823, where one of his greatest achievements was to found the town's first free library. He published *The Moral Social and Religious Condition of Ipswich* ... in 1850, *The New Suffolk Garland* in 1866, and *Illustrations of Old Ipswich* in 1889. Ipswich's archives would be immeasurably poorer without him.

Kathleen Hale

Hale, like **Ronald Blythe**, lived right through the twentieth century, dying at the age of 101 in 2000. Her gloriously bright and cheerful illustrations for the *Orlando* books, with all their sly wit and subtle social commentary, owed much to the expertise of the Ipswich printer, W. S. Cowell, of the same family that produced Edward Byles Cowell, the man who suggested the translation of the *Rubaiyat* to **Edward FitzGerald**. Hale herself came to know Suffolk through the circle of painters around Cedrick Morris and his partner Arthur Lett-Haines at Higham, then at Dedham, then at Benton End outside Hadleigh. Others in the same circle included Maggi Hambling and Lucian Freud. You live long enough, especially in Suffolk, all the lines eventually connect.

It's been suggested that Hale put herself into the character of Orlando's black kitten, Twinkle. I do hope that's true.

Maggie Hemingway

Born in Orford, Maggie Hemingway published four novels before her all-too-early death in 1993. The inner life of her characters is observed with the same care Hemingway brings to her descriptions of landscape; she is clinical in depicting how one works upon the other. The countryside and coastline around Walberswick in Queen Victoria's Golden Jubilee Year of 1887 depicted in *The Bridge* has changed very little, despite the worst the North Sea could do, but as to which bridge is in the painting, and which it was in the book, you must decide for yourself.

Patricia Highsmith

Born in Texas in 1921, Suffolk was the setting for one short chapter in Highsmith's restless and complicated life, but it was the stepping stone that took her across the Atlantic to base herself permanently in Europe for the rest of her life. Memories of the frenetic and unhappy love affair that brought her first to Aldeburgh, in 1963, then to Earl Soham, no doubt hide in the underbelly of many of her later works. A happier outcome was her friendship and correspondence with **Ronald Blythe**, which continued until her death in 1995.

Francis Hindes Groome

Hindes Groome (1851–1902) is described in the *Dictionary of National Biography* as 'A singularly alert, swift, and eager intellect, he was unwearied in research, impatient of anything less than precision, a frank and fearless critic'. He developed the fascination with Roma folklore and the Romany way of life that would lead to his major works while still an Ipswich schoolboy. From 1877 he also edited 'Suffolk Notes and Queries' in the *Ipswich Journal*.

Anthony Horowitz

Horowitz has written mysteries and thrillers for adults, for children, and for TV, and has adopted the personas of Ian Fleming and Sir Arthur Conan Doyle to add to their literary canon. His trilogy of Suffolk murder-mysteries (beginning with *Magpie Murders* in 2016), featuring the much put-upon editor Susan Ryeland and her author Alan Conway, and Conway's *fictional* detective Atticus Pünd, are a delight – dancing about the reader, dropping their veils on every page, yet always with one more mystery, one more twist to reveal.

Elizabeth Inchbald

Born Elizabeth Simpson in the village of Stanningfield on the River Lark, some 5 miles (8 kilometres) from Bury St Edmunds, in 1753, she was the eighth of nine children. Having been educated at home, perhaps because she had a stammer, or perhaps because she was a daughter, not a son, at the age of eighteen she left Stanningfield to follow her brother George onto the stage. After two months on her own in London Elizabeth was so exhausted by the predatory attention she received that she married Joseph Inchbald, an actor who was twice her age, and for the next seven years toured with him. On Inchbald's death, she supported herself as a playwright and novelist. Her novel *A Simple Story* is a cross-generational family epic, much concerned with questions of religious freedom (the Simpson family was Catholic), women's rights, personal morality and social inequality. Lytton Strachey was a fan; Elizabeth, who died in Kensington in 1821, has also been championed by feminist scholars today.

Stanningfield itself is a perfect example of one of those Suffolk villages with a smaller population now than it had 200 years ago – or at least it was, until it twinned itself with nearby Bradfield Combust in 1988. Despite their tiny size, both villages have an impressive array of listed buildings and historic places of interest. **Will Kempe** danced through Bradfield Combust, and Stanningfield was home to the Catholic Ambrose Rookwood, one of the Gunpowder Plotters.

Hammond Innes

'A writer has no business, no land, no factory that he can call his own. His capital assets are all in his head, and one of the very few things that can't be taxed, expropriated, or in any way filched by others, is personal experience,' said Innes in 1972. Born in Sussex in 1913, Innes originally worked as a journalist, served in the Royal Artillery in the Second World War, and truly began his series of thrillers in 1948 with *Maddon's Rock*. He had the knack of creating everyman heroes who are called upon to be extraordinary, and the kind of writing practise most of us can only weep for – six months' research, six months of writing, and a new book almost every year, ready for the Christmas market. He was a dedicated environmentalist as well, when such were very few. Innes died in 1988 at the age of eighty-four.

Henry James

James (1843–1916) visited Suffolk in 1897 and became fascinated by Dunwich and its fate, as were so many of his fellow Victorians. His essay 'Old Suffolk' was published in *English Hours*, his anthology of his English travel writing, in 1905. I've always found it intriguing that *The Turn of the Screw* came out the year after James's Dunwich visit. Did the eerie atmosphere of Dunwich, which had so many more of its ruins intact when James visited than it does today, play a part in the colouring of that story?

M. R. James

As a writer of ghost stories, M. R. James (1862–1936) stands between the generation of Victorian writers such as Sheridan Le Fanu and just about everyone who has come after. His formula was so simple – a place, a person, and a thing – but it has hardly been bettered since. He augmented this with his own knowledge as a medievalist of note – his research led to the discovery of the lost graves of three abbots known to **Jocelin of Brakelond** at Bury St Edmunds, for example.

His first ghost stories were told to the select few, in time-honoured fashion, as Christmas entertainments round James's own fireside, but as soon as the first were published, in 1904, readers were clamouring for more. Five collections of his stories, including an omnibus edition, appeared in his lifetime.

P. D. James

P. D. James (1920–2014) gave her detective hero Adam Dalgliesh a beloved aunt with a cottage at 'Monksmere' on the Suffolk coast, close by James's own holiday home of Southwold, thus bringing art and life into one. When interviewed in 2001, she said 'I have a house on the coast at Suffolk – that's really where I can do my best plotting, because *I can walk along the sand* [my italics] and think and plot and get in touch with my characters. I love, I suppose, the great skies, the emptiness of it, I just love being by the sea.' She was a great lover of the melancholy atmosphere of Dunwich, too. And she named the woman who finally wins Dalgliesh's heart 'Emma Lavenham'.

Jocelin of Brakelond

Jocelin was an English Benedictine monk, whose *Chronicle of the Abbey of St Edmunds* covers the years 1173–1202, during the abbacy first of Hugo, then of Samson of Tottington, a Norfolk man whose abbacy improved the fortunes of the Abbey no end. Jocelin's loyalty to and admiration for Abbot Samson colour every word of the *Chronicle*. Think of him as a twelfth-century COO – dutiful and diligent, with a horror of debt and mismanagement, and as a faithful recorder of all the backstairs politicking and public manoeuvring necessary in the administration of so great a religious house. The most recent edition of his *Chronicle* came out in 1989; a 1903 edition can be found at Project Gutenberg.

Will Kempe

Kempe was born *c.*1560, and by 1585 was a member of the Earl of Leicester's group of players. His reputation for physical comedy, especially the onstage 'jig', or comic dance, grew throughout the 1580s and roles were shaped up to favour his skills and play on his popularity. By 1594 he was one of the Lord Chamberlain's men, along with Richard Burbage and

Shakespeare himself, playing Dogberry in *Much Ado About Nothing* and perhaps the Gravedigger in *Hamlet*, but by 1599 there had been a falling-out; Kempe left the company and embarked on his *Nine Days' Wonder* in the spring of 1600 as a means of generating publicity for a solo career. During this (it lasted several weeks rather than just nine days) he 'jigged' or otherwise danced from London to Norwich and became something of a celebrity: crowds turned out to watch and cheer, and occasionally, as we have seen, to join in. His account of his 'Wonder' was published to prove he had actually done it, and in it, Kempe records dancing in Long Melford, Clare, and Bury, as well as with that 'Country Lass, brown as a berry' in Sudbury.

Sadly the 'Wonder' does not seem to have revived Kempe's career for long, and in about 1603 he disappears from the records. He may have died in that year (one of London's plague years) in Southwark, but the *Nine Days' Wonder* survives at Project Gutenberg.

John Kirby

Kirby was born in Halesworth in 1690, worked as a schoolmaster in Orford, and later lived in Wickham Market, where he wrote his *Suffolk Traveller* between 1732 and 1734, publishing it in Ipswich in 1735, complete with a map of the country. He was a pioneer in the field of topography, a profession in which he was followed by his son, Joshua. Both father and son were painted by Gainsborough, who was an especially close friend of Joshua's, who in turn became known for his teachings on perspective. John Kirby's *Suffolk Traveller* is online at the Internet Archive. He died in Ipswich 1753.

Norah Lofts

Born in Norfolk in 1904, Lofts came to Bury St Edmunds as a schoolgirl and was to make it the centre of her professional and creative life, hiding it in her writing as the town of 'Baildon'. Along with the historical fiction for which she was famous on both sides of the Atlantic, she also wrote mysteries and short stories. There are characteristic Loftsian effects in her writing: for example, individuals loop in and out of her plots from one book to the next; rural poverty is never sugar-coated; evil is punished, but not without compassion. Several of her more than fifty novels were turned into films, one by John Ford. So good and so steady a storyteller was she that two new titles by her could be published even after her death at the age of seventy-nine in 1983.

John Lydgate

Lydgate (*c.*1370-*c.*1451) entered the Benedictine monastery of Bury St Edmunds at the age of twelve or so, eventually becoming prior of Hatfield Broad Oak in Essex. In 1423 he resigned from the Church and spent the rest of his life travelling and writing. A great admirer of Geoffrey Chaucer, he modelled a number of his poems on Chaucer's works. They do not shine in comparison, and the older Lydgate got, the longer he wrote, which is rarely a good thing, but he does seem to have been the first to coin the adage 'needs must when the devil drives'. In his old age he retired to Bury St Edmunds, at which time he may have left a somewhat mysterious Latin graffito in the church of St Mary's, Lidgate, discovered in only 2014. His poems 'Testament' and 'Lamentation of our Lady Maria' are painted along the roof and west wall of the Clopton Chantry Chapel in Holy Trinity Church, Long Melford. Go see them, and unite yourself with the Clopton family, Lydgate, and **Robert Louis Stevenson** in one fell swoop. Also, somehow, the stained glass in the church escaped the attention of **William Dowsing** and his myrmidons. It more than repays a visit. Many of Lydgate's work are online at the Internet Archive.

Joseph McCabe

McCabe (1867–1955) was a Catholic novitiate and priest, but lost his religious beliefs in the 1880s and become a rationalist and secular humanist – which no doubt assisted his friendship with **Edward Clodd** and saw him granted the role of Clodd's biographer. He also championed women's rights, derided spiritualism, and came off somewhat the worst in a literary spat with G. K. Chesterton, as detailed in Chesterton's *Heretics*.

Noreen Masud

Masud came to Scotland with her British mother at the age of fifteen after a scarifyingly strange childhood in Pakistan. Her book *A Flat Place* (2023) is an unpacking of herself within moorland, fields, and the alien-seeming surroundings of Orford Ness on the Suffolk coast: a search for form and sense and logic in victimhood in places that give undemanding space for memory.

It says much, I think, of what the Suffolk landscape is, and the qualities it has, that it can reach into and comfort so diversely.

Edward Moor

Moor (1771–1848), **Edward FitzGerald**'s childhood friend, retired to Great Bealings in Suffolk in 1806 after a military career with the East India Company and published *Suffolk Words and Phrases* in 1823. *Bealing Bells*, published in 1841, describes his experience of what he claimed to be, or believed to be, poltergeist activity where the servants' bells in Bealings House, his home, rang for fifty-three days. It is equally possible that Moor staged the whole thing for his own amusement; certainly, the man behind *Suffolk Words and*

Phrases had the right gently subversive sense of humour to have done so.

Julie Myerson

Another who first came to Suffolk as a child; another who has used Southwold and Walberswick as fictionalised backdrops to her writing. *The Stopped Heart* (2016) is supernaturally good at evoking how, in Suffolk, the past never really goes away. Also, if you are in need of another example of how all life becomes grist to the writer's mill, how nothing stops us processing everything about us, Myerson is it. 'Once they've started, that's it,' one of her characters declares, 'they'll go to any lengths to find the right words.'

Ouida

The astoundingly prolific Ouida (Marie Louise Ramé) was born in 1839 in Bury St Edmunds to an English mother and a French father and died in Italy in 1908. After the publication of *Under Two Flags* in 1867 (maybe the first novel in which the hero runs away to join the Foreign Legion) she moved into the Langham Hotel in London where she apparently wrote in bed by candlelight, and held soirées in which she entertained Oscar Wilde, **Algernon Swinburne**, and **Wilkie Collins**, among many others. Moving to Italy around 1871 she lived first of all in Florence, then in Bagni di

Lucca, maintaining the most opulent of lifestyles for as long as she could. A ferocious campaigner for animal rights (she was described as having a voice 'like a carving knife'), she is commemorated in her birthplace with a drinking fountain for horses and dogs. Her *A Dog of Flanders* was adapted for film as recently as 1999.

George Orwell

The man who conjured up *1984* and *Animal Farm* did not, I think, much care for Suffolk, at least at first. His parents retired to Southwold so that his father could play golf and because the town was populated by people just like them ('lower-upper middle class', was how their son anathematised them). Eric Blair (as was) joined them there on leaving the Burmese police, but decamped to Portobello, then to Paris, as soon as he could. He was back in 1927 working as a private tutor, as a teacher, and to learn himself the business of how to be a writer. Whether he liked it or not, Southwold was somewhere he came back to over and over again until a final move to London in 1934. *Down and Out in Paris and London* was published in 1933, *Burmese Days* in 1934, then *A Clergyman's Daughter* in 1935, and so George Orwell (1903–50) was launched.

Robert Reyce (or Ryece)

Reyce's family were first recorded in the village of Preston St Mary in the fifteenth century. Preston is another tiny village out in the green, a little north of Monks Eleigh and Brent Eleigh; Reyce (1555–1638) and his wife Mary are both buried in the village church. Reyce's family owned the manor house and his father was a JP, and Ryece was able to make a name as an antiquary, with the leisure to write, all of which demonstrates that the family were well-to-do. Indeed, all the way through the *Breviary*, the tone is that of a man wholly content with his life and quietly in love with his native land. He details everything from the air of Suffolk to its crops, its livestock, and its songbirds, its roads, its architecture, and its nobility; its churches and its 'learned men' (such as Lydgate).

Reyce completed his *Breviary of Suffolk* in 1618, but it only saw the light of day in 1902, complete with more than 100 pages of notes from Lord Francis Hervey, one-time MP for Bury St Edmunds. There is a lesson for all who think they will never be published. It is available through archive.org.

Rebecca Ribbans

Ribbans was born in Lavenham in 1795, married Frederick Ribbans, the local schoolmaster, and died there in 1821, very possibly in childbirth. A little life we might know nothing of at all, were it not for Hugh McKeon's *Historical Notes and Observations ... of the Parish of Lavenham* of 1826, and for the words of her husband when he had 'Lavenham Church' printed in her memory in 1822: 'Serene, satisfied and sanguine in the hopes of eternal happiness, her departure from this life resembled the mellow calmness, the mild tranquillity of an Autumnal evening ...'

Morley Roberts

Roberts (1857–1942), friend of **Edward Clodd**, was a prolific writer of fiction and non-fiction, who sailed steerage to Australia at the age of nineteen and later travelled to South Africa and Oceania. His travels form the basis of much of his writing, which feature a cast of wanderers, adventurers, miners, and jackaroos, pitting themselves against the worst that the wilderness and their fellow men could throw at them. Several of his works are available at Project Gutenberg.

W. G. Sebald

Winfried George ('Max') Sebald came to East Anglia in 1970 as a lecturer at the University of East Anglia. You can't categorise him as anything that existed until he himself started writing – thoughts that wander where they will, turn back upon themselves, interconnect and pass on into something else; prose that is fiction, travel writing, memoir – all of these, and none of them. *The Rings of Saturn* commemorates a walk around Suffolk in the dog days of August, and as ever with

Sebald's writing, is concerned with themes of time and dissolution – as was the Roman god. This probably has nothing to do with Sebald's choice of title.

There is a philosophical melancholy to Sebald's writing which has always seemed to me to reflect the fact that he knew he had a serious heart defect, one that would likely kill him before his time. It did: at the age of fifty-seven in 2001.

Clement King Shorter

Shorter (1857–1926) founded and edited *The Tatler*, as well as editing *The Illustrated London News*. *Immortal Memories* gives just a hint of how trenchant his opinions could be as a critic, but no hint of his enthusiasm for the writing of the Brontë sisters, which makes this rather self-opinionated man rather more appealing – as does his marriage to the Irish poet Dora Sigerson.

Stevie Smith

Smith's older sister Molly moved to Suffolk after their mother's death in 1919; the poet visited her there and was moved to compose 'The River Deben'.

Stevie Smith (1902–71) has been called the poet of quiet desperation, but after years of unreliable health from childhood on, the inevitability of death seems to have been more of a source of comfort to her than despair. You wonder if her deeply personal relationship with rivers and seas and water of all sorts might have been influenced by the fact that her father ran away to sea when she was only three.

Algernon Charles Swinburne

Swinburne was born in 1837 and came to Suffolk in the 1870s, apparently at the behest of Theodore Watts-Dunton – himself a friend and correspondent of **Edward Clodd** and **Francis Hindes Groome**. Swinburne was writing to Edmund Gosse from South House, on the South Green at Southwold in 1875, having been brought or sent there by Watts-Dunton in one of his many interventions in Swinburne's lifestyle, which by then had shaded from the self-consciously outrageous to the wholly self-destructive. *By the North Sea* followed in 1880, by which time Swinburne was living with Watts-Dunton in Putney, where he was to remain until his death in 1909.

Robert Louis Stevenson

Oh, how I would love to have known Stevenson (1850–94). A family wedding brought him to Suffolk in 1870; on his return in 1873, while staying with his cousin Maud Babington at Cockfield Rectory, he met and fell deeply in love with Fanny Sitwell, a friend of his cousin. Sitwell was unhappily married herself at the time; once widowed she would eventually marry Sidney Colvin, who was to see to the publication of Stevenson's essay 'Roads' in the monthly magazine *The Portfolio* in the same year. The roads of Suffolk roll all the way through the essay, Stevenson's first published work; likewise, the lightness and excitement of being newly and ecstatically in love.

J. E. Vincent

James Edmund Vincent (1857–1909) was a Welshman by birth. A barrister, author, and journalist, he joined the staff of *The Times* in 1886. He wrote a couple of royal biographies, an early history of the game of football, and a history of the River Thames, but *Through East Anglia in a Motor Car* remains the book for which he was best known.

The Books

In addition to the books detailed here, I also found myself returning to two recent anthologies: *A Distant Cry*, with a foreword by Louis de Bernières, published by Black Dog Books in 2002; and *A New Suffolk Garland*, published by the Boydell Press in 2022.

Titles given here but now out of print can all be found online via the Internet Archive, Project Gutenberg, or WorldCat.

Kerri Andrews, *Wanderers: A History of Women Walking* (Reaktion, 2020)

Adrian Bell, The Rural Trilogy:
Corduroy (Cobden-Sanderson, 1930);
Silver Ley (Cobden-Sanderson, 1931);
The Cherry Tree (Cobden-Sanderson, 1932)

Robert Bloomfield, *The Farmer's Boy* (Vernon Hood, 1800)

James Blyth, *Edward FitzGerald and Posh* (John Long, 1908)

Ronald Blythe, *Akenfield: Portrait of an English Village* (Allen Lane, 1969)

———, *The Time by the Sea* (Faber & Faber, 2013)
Edward Clodd, *A Guide to Aldeburgh* (J. Buck, 1861)
William Cobbett, *Rural Rides* (*The Political Register*, 1822–6)
Henry Cockton, *The Life and Adventures of Valentine Vox* (Robert Tyas, 1840)
———, *Lady Felicia* (Office of the National Illustrated Library, 1852)
Wilkie Collins, *No Name* (Sampson Low, Son, and Marston, 1862)
George Crabbe, *The Borough* (J. Hatchard, 1810)
Daniel Defoe, *Tour Thro' the Whole Island of Great Britain* (George Strahan, 1724–7)
Charles Dickens, *The Pickwick Papers* (Chapman & Hall, 1837)
William Dowsing, *Journal* (1643–4; definitive edition by the Boydell Press, 2001)
William Alfred Dutt, *Literary Associations of East Anglia* (Methuen, 1907)
George Ewart Evans, *The Pattern Under the Plough* (Faber, 1966)
Edward FitzGerald (trans.), *The Rubaiyat of Omar Khayyam* (translated 1858; illustrated edition by Hodder & Stoughton, 1909)
———, *Sea Words and Phrases* (Samuel Tymme, 1870)
———, *Letters* (W. Aldis Wright, 1889)

Penelope Fitzgerald, *The Bookshop* (Gerald Duckworth, 1978)

Esther Freud, *The Sea House* (Hamish Hamilton, 2003)

John Glyde, *Life of Edward Fitz-Gerald* (C. A. Pearson, 1900)

Maggie Hemingway, *The Bridge* (Jonathan Cape, 1986)

Patricia Highsmith, *A Suspension of Mercy* (Heinemann, 1965)

Anthony Horowitz, Susan Ryeland series:
Magpie Murders (Orion, 2016);
Moonflower Murders (Century, 2020);
Marble Hall Murders (Century, 2025)

Francis Hindes Groome, *Two Suffolk Friends* (William Blackwood and Sons, 1895)

Elizabeth Inchbald, *Nature and Art* (P. Wogan, P. Byrne et al., 1786)

———, *A Simple Story* (G. G. J. & J. Robinson, 1791)

Hammond Innes, *Hammond Innes' East Anglia* (Hodder & Stoughton, 1986)

M. R. James, *Suffolk and Norfolk* (J. M. Dent & Sons, 1930)

———, 'Oh, Whistle, and I'll Come to You, My Lad' (1904); 'The Tractate Middoth' (1911); 'Mr Humphreys and His Inheritance' (1911); 'A Warning to the Curious' (1925) in *The Collected Ghost Stories of M. R. James* (Edward Arnold, 1931)

P. D. James, *Unnatural Causes* (Faber & Faber, 1967)

———, *Devices and Desires* (Faber & Faber, 1989)

——————, *The Children of Men* (Faber & Faber, 1992)
Jocelin of Brakelond, *Chronicle of the Abbey of St Edmunds* (*c.*1200; published in English by Whittaker & Co., 1844)
William Kempe, *Nine Days' Wonder* (1600; republished by The Camden Society, 1839)
John Kirby, *Suffolk Traveller* (1735; second edition published by J. Shave, 1764)
Norah Lofts, The Suffolk Trilogy:
The Town House (Hutchinson & Co., 1959);
The House at Old Vine (Hutchinson & Co., 1961);
The House at Sunset (Hutchinson & Co., 1963)
John Lydgate, 'Kalendare' (collected in *The Minor Poems of John Lydgate* for The Early English Text Society, 1911)
——————, *Lives of Ss Edmund & Fremund* and the *Extra Miracles of St Edmund* (republished by Universitatverlag Winter, 2009)
Noreen Masud, *A Flat Place* (Melville House, 2023)
Edward Moor, *Suffolk Words and Phrases* (John Loder, 1823)
——————, *Bealings Bells* (John Loder, 1841)
Julie Myerson, *Something Might Happen* (Jonathan Cape, 2003)
——————, *The Stopped Heart* (Jonathan Cape, 2016)
George Orwell, *A Clergyman's Daughter* (Victor Gollancz, 1935)
Ouida, *Two Little Wooden Shoes* (Bernhard Tauchnitz, 1874)

Ruth Rendell, *The Brimstone Wedding* (Viking, 1996)
Robert Reyce, *Breviary of Suffolk* (1618; published by John Murray, 1902)
Rebecca Ribbans, 'Lavenham Church' (The County Press, 1822)
W. G. Sebald, *The Rings of Saturn* (1995; published in English by New Directions, 1998)
Clement King Shorter, *Immortal Memories* (Harper & Brothers, 1907)
Robert Louis Stevenson, 'Roads' (*The Portfolio*, 1873)
J. E. Vincent, *Through East Anglia in a Motor Car* (Methuen, 1907)

Acknowledgements

First of all, I have to thank my indefatigable companions on these walks – Barbara, Mark, and Hans. May all our wanderings together be so happy.

The team at Haus, who are as ever models of how it should be done: Harry, Ed, Maddie, Edoardo, and Luz; and my agent Chelsey Fox.

Some specific thanks for information garnered and most gratefully received: the magnificent British Library; Paul Lewis and his website for information on Wilkie Collins in Aldeburgh; and Narguess Farzad for answering my questions on Edward FitzGerald.

Going back to the surroundings of one's childhood makes one thoughtful. I would like to record here the debt I owe to a particular teacher, Miss Ruff of Ipswich High School GPDST, who first set me on the path of reading as many books as I could get my hands on, and ultimately of writing them as well.

And all the many splendid Suffolk bookshops – independents, second-hand, and chains both great and small – without which the idea for this book would never have suggested itself, and it certainly couldn't have been written.